CRUMBS FROM THE MASTER'S TABLE

CRUMBS

FROM THE

MASTER'S TABLE

OR, SELECT SENTENCES,

DOCTRINAL, PRACTICAL, AND EXPERIMENTAL

BY

WILLIAM MASON

CURIOSMITH

MINNEAPOLIS

2012

Published by Curiosmith.
P. O. Box 390293, Minneapolis, Minnesota, 55439.
Internet: curiosmith.com.
E-mail: shopkeeper@curiosmith.com.

All scripture quotations are from *The Holy Bible*, King James version.

Previously printed and sold by J. Matthews in 1792.

Supplementary content and cover design:
Copyright © 2012 Charles J. Doe.

ISBN 9781935626480

CRUMBS FROM THE MASTER'S TABLE

———◆◇◆———

WOULD you enjoy much of the comfort of faith, read and meditate much the word of faith: and look constantly to Jesus, the author and finisher of faith. HEBREWS 12:2.

We may be sure we possess the faith of God's elect, if we submit to Christ's righteousness for justification unto life; and have respect unto all his commands, for obedience unto righteousness. ROMANS 6:16.

If strong confidence abounds in the heart without obedience unto Christ in the life, sin blinds the conscience, and Satan deludes the soul. Be not deceived: God is not mocked. GALATIANS 6:7.

Sin will be always stirring; therefore we must be constantly striving, continually watching, always praying, and ever looking unto Jesus. HEBREWS 12:2.

It is the vilest of all sins, to make Christ the minister of sin: as though we were to take license to sin, because his grace has abounded over sin to salvation. Shall we continue in sin, that grace may abound? God forbid. ROMANS 6:1.

Free grace is the poor sinner's plea; the free salvation of Christ, his glory; that it is by free gift of free promise, his triumph. Lord, enable me daily to live as a poor pensioner upon thy free bounty. Thy grace is exceeding abundant. 1 TIMOTHY 1:14.

When we pray for faith, or the increase of faith in God's word, we honor the God of truth, and he will honor us: for saith the Lord, Them that honor me, I will honor. 1 SAMUEL 2:30.

It is a shame to profess to believe the doctrines of grace, and yet be ashamed to confess them; for saith Christ, Whosoever shall be ashamed of me and of my words, of him shall the Son of man be ashamed. LUKE 9:26.

Though we have not the Spirit always to bear witness with our spirits that we are the children of God, yet he always bears witness in the word, that Jesus is the Son of God, and that all who believe on him are the children of God, reconciled to God, and at peace with God. The faith of this excites hope, and encourages prayer in the poor sinner's heart, that the God of hope would fill him with all joy and peace in believing, by the power of the Holy Ghost. ROMANS 15:13.

When a sinner prays, Lord Jesus, save, or I perish, the Spirit hath inspired that cry in his heart, which he will never lose but with his expiring breath. Hear the testimony of the Spirit: Whosoever shall call upon the name of the Lord, shall be saved. ROMANS 10:13.

He who aims to fulfil the law for justification, despises the gospel, rejects Christ's righteousness, and is under the condemnation of the law and the wrath of justice for his unbelief. JOHN 3:36.

Though we shall not be saved *for* our holiness, yet we are saved *unto* holiness, and are kept in the way *of* holiness to eternal glory. The more we believe the truth, the more we are sanctified through the truth, and enjoy more of the God of truth by faith: the more enjoyment of God, the more holiness from God. With open face beholding in the glass of the gospel the glory of the Lord, we are changed into the same image, from glory to glory, by the Spirit of the Lord. 2 CORINTHIANS 3:18.

We cannot keep ourselves. Be humble. God has promised to keep us by his power unto salvation. Be joyful. But forget not we are kept through faith. 1 PETER 1:5. In all your dejections, consult the word of faith. ROMANS 10:8. In all your weakness, look unto Jesus, the author and finisher of faith. HEBREWS 12:2. Be ever looking from yourself, ever going out of self; ever coming up out of nature's wilderness, leaning upon your Beloved. SONG OF SOLOMON 8:5.

When tempted to seek happiness in and comfort from the things of this life, remember Christ is our life. COLOSSIANS 3:4. In him we have all things, and abound. Turn from earthly shadows to Christ your heavenly substance, and appeal to him: There is none upon earth that I desire besides thee. PSALM 73:25. This choice pleaseth him. He will comfort you.

Though we cannot bring a lively frame of soul to God, yet a dead one should not keep us from him; for Christ our life is ever the same to us, we are ever alike accepted in him, He is ever before the throne for us. HEBREWS 8:1.

When you find yourself weak, your frame bad, your spirits low, your prospects dreary, and your enemies powerful, this is the very time to honor and obey your Lord's sweet invitations: Look unto me. ISAIAH 45:22. Come unto me. MATTHEW 11:28. Call upon me in the day of trouble: I will deliver thee, and thou shalt glorify me. PSALM 50:15.

We can never walk comfortably with God, unless we see by faith that his holy law is perfectly fulfilled for us by Christ, God perfectly reconciled to us in Christ, and at perfect peace with us through the blood of Christ. Faith receives the comfort of all this from the word, and returns God all the glory according to the word: My glory I will not give to another. ISAIAH 42:8. Teach me thy way, O Lord; I will walk in thy truth. PSALM 86:11.

Soul complaints under the burden of sin are full evidences that Christ is the life of the soul. Groaning under the lustings of the flesh, as preventing us from living more to the Lord, is a full proof that we have his Spirit, which lusteth against the flesh. GALATIANS 5:17. Who maketh thee to differ from another? 1 CORINTHIANS 4:7.

Would you be established in grace? Study much the covenant of grace, established from eternity by Father, Son, and Spirit. From hence flow peace with God the Father, redemption by God the Son, and consolation from God the Spirit, to haters of God, enemies to God, and rebels against God. Be not carried about with divers and strange doctrines; for it is a good thing that the heart be established with grace. HEBREWS 13:9. Lord, show me thy covenant. PSALM 25:14.

Faith gives freedom of access to God, and boldness in prayer before God; for it looks to Christ's finished work on earth, and to his mediation and intercession in heaven: and God is ever well pleased with his beloved Son, and perfectly reconciled to sinners in him. 2 CORINTHIANS 5:19.

To deny the Spirit's work on the heart betrays ignorance of experimental knowledge of Christ in the heart. We as much need the Spirit to enlighten, convince, convert, and sanctify us, as the atonement and righteousness of Christ to justify and save us. Is Christ glorious in our eyes, and precious to our hearts? Whom may we thank for it? Jesus tells us, The Spirit shall glorify me. He shall receive of mine, and shall show it unto you. JOHN 16:14. What the word of truth testifies of Christ, the Spirit of truth causes us to believe, and he enables us to follow Christ. God the Spirit, who began, fulfils the work of faith with power in our hearts on earth, till we see Jesus in glory. 2 THESSALONIANS 1:11.

By human art men kill the life of quicksilver: by the arts of the adversary professors kill the spirit and life of Christ's words, so as to destroy their effects on them. Take one instance for a thousand: Christ commands, Lay not up for yourselves treasures upon earth. MATTHEW 6:19. Covetousness can so qualify this word, that professors can lay up riches in life, and leave behind them many thousands at their death, while thousands of Christ's members want necessaries. Thus thousands deceive themselves with a notion that they are Christ's friends, while they aim to make him a liar. For he says, Ye are my friends, if ye do whatsoever I command you. JOHN 15:14. Consider this deeply: The love of money is the root of all evil. 1 TIMOTHY 6:10. Covetousness is idolatry. COLOSSIANS 3:5. Ye know that no idolater hath any inheritance in the kingdom of Christ and of God. EPHESIANS 5:5. Lord, keep me from trifling with thy solemn truths.

Invert not the order of the gospel. Our fruits of righteousness do not make us righteous. Our fruit unto holiness doth not make us holy; but being united unto Christ, we bring forth fruit unto God. ROMANS 7:4. Being made righteous in Christ, we bring forth the fruits of righteousness, which are by Christ. PHILIPPIANS 1:11. Being sanctified in Christ, and called to be saints of Christ, we have our fruit unto holiness, and the end everlasting life. ROMANS 6:22. If the root be holy, so are the branches. Yet boast not of thy fruit, but glory in Christ thy root; for if thou boast, thou bearest not the root, but the root thee. ROMANS 11:18. Corrupt minds, of no judgment concerning the faith, resist the truth. 2 TIMOTHY 3:8. Lord, give me understanding in all things. 2 TIMOTHY 2:7.

Look within yourself, and at your best works, and you will see enough for humiliation. Look into the word of grace and truth which came by Jesus Christ, and you will see enough for consolation. Lord, let me never forget that by thy free favor I am saved through faith. EPHESIANS 2:8.

Think not that you have an inherent stock of grace in yourself. The thought elates with pride, blinds to our own nothingness, opposes faith in Christ, prevents our coming to Christ, and receiving out of the fullness of the grace of Christ. He feedeth the hungry with good things; the rich he sendeth empty away. LUKE 1:53.

Chastisements and afflictions are covenant blessings in disguise from the heart of a God of love, and from the hand of a God of mercy. Hereby the God of wisdom chastens his beloved children from the love of sin to the love of Christ, who hath put away our sins by the sacrifice of himself. HEBREWS 9:26. Hear ye the rod, and who hath appointed it. MICAH 6:9.

Christ has finished salvation for lost sinners. Who shall enjoy the comfort of it now, and the fullness of it in eternity? Every one who believes in him, and works out his own salvation with fear and trembling. Lord, work in me both to will and to do, of thine own good pleasure. PHILIPPIANS 2:12, 13.

There is not a clearer truth under heaven than this: ALL may be saved by Christ who will: ALL shall find salvation in Christ who will come to him for it. JOHN 6:37. O my soul, hast thou a will to be saved; to be saved by Jesus;

to be saved from sin and self-righteous pride, as well as from hell; into holiness, as well as into heaven? then never indulge a doubt of thy salvation. Rejoice always in Christ thy Savior. Give God all the glory, who made thee willing in the day of his power. PSALM 110:3.

Who will show us any good? To this inquiry Paul answers briefly, PUT YE ON THE LORD JESUS CHRIST. ROMANS 13:14. There is not one good out of Christ. There is every good in him. Prove this constantly, ye who believe in him. Put him on afresh, in your mind, memory, and conscience, and you shall joyfully say, with Paul, I have all, and abound; I am full. PHILIPPIANS 4:18.

He who neglects to watch will be sure to smart for it. He who thinks he has got above duty, and beyond his Lord's command to all, *Watch*, will soon find, like Samson, that the Lord is departed from him; that the enemies will come upon him, put out his eyes, set him to grind in the mill, and make sport of him for his folly. Though God has promised to keep us, yet it will be only in that way he has prescribed, even in obedience to his will. Lord, suffer me neither to tempt thee by wilful disobedience, nor to distrust thee by woeful unbelief.

The blood of the Son of God cleanseth us from all sin. 1 JOHN 1:7. Therefore every believing sinner in Christ is, in God's sight, as pure and as clean from all sin, as though he had never sinned. But he is to be holding this mystery of faith in a pure conscience. 1 TIMOTHY 3:9. Where the love of Jesus reigns, the guilt of sin is removed, the dominion of sin dethroned, self-righteousness abhorred, and the heart says, Lord, I esteem all thy precepts concerning all things to be right; and I hate every false way. PSALM 119:128.

He who is under the law, is like one married to a wife

whom he hates, and who also hates him. She neither gives him a good word nor a pleasant look; but with a froward face continually commands him, Work, work, do, do; and after all his working and doing, laboring and toiling, only rates and abuses him with, Cursed art thou; for thou hast not continued in all things which are written in the book of the law to do them. GALATIANS 3:10. The contentions of such a wife, are a continual dropping. PROVERBS 19:13.

A prudent man will ride a vicious horse with care, keep a watchful eye over him, and a tight rein upon him, to prevent evil. So a wise Christian, who is taught the many tricks of his desperately deceitful and deplorably wicked heart, will obey the command of the Holy Ghost: Keep thy heart with all diligence, PROVERBS 4:23, lest it stumble in the way of truth, kick at the sacrifice of Christ, rear up with pride and self-righteousness, or run away into the broad road of worldly cares, carnal pleasures, or self-pleasing gratifications, so as, with Jeshurun, to forsake the God who made him, and lightly esteem JESUS, the Rock of his salvation. DEUTERONOMY 32:15.

The knowledge of our own character as sinners, and that of Jesus Christ the RIGHTEOUS, taught by the word of truth, are the chief points in Christianity. By the former, we sink into self-despair. By the latter, we rise into the happy enjoyment of God, holy fellowship with God, sweet peace from God, heavenly joy in God, pleasing delight to obey God, and longing hope to enjoy God. Our dear Lord says, That which ye have already, hold fast till I come. REVELATION 2:25.

Why is our salvation ascribed to faith? Because, believing in Christ, we come to him for all, employ him in all, trust him through all, look to him under all, hope in him to do all, from him expect all, and to him ascribe the glory of all. Jesus honors faith above all, because it honors him and his truth above all; making him the all-in-all of our salvation. Build up yourselves in your most holy faith. JUDE 20.

John the Baptist was great in the sight of the Lord. LUKE 1:15. But he was little in his own eyes. MARK 1:7. Just so it is with every poor sinner who is favored with the grace of Jesus. For when the day of the Lord of hosts comes upon us who are naturally lifted up, we shall be brought low, and the Lord alone shall be exalted in that day. ISAIAH 2:11. In the valley of humility is the vision of joy.

How shall I know that I am born of God? Our Lord gives a more infallible proof than if an angel from heaven had answered you: He who is of God, heareth God's words. JOHN 8:47. He understands, believes, and loves them. Mind how God himself honors his own word of inspiration, when he spoke from heaven this testimony of Jesus: This is my beloved Son, in whom I am well pleased. MATTHEW 3:17. He uses the words of three Old Testament texts: This is my beloved Son. PSALM 2:7. In whom I am well pleased. ISAIAH 42:1. Hear ye him. DEUTERONOMY 18:15. Here is both proof of the divinity of Scripture, and of your being of God, if you receive God's testimony into your heart by faith, that the man Jesus is God's Son, the only Savior: for whosoever believeth that Jesus is the Christ, the anointed Savior, is born of God. 1 JOHN 5:1. Whosoever shall confess that Jesus is the Son of God, God dwelleth in him, and he in God. 1 JOHN 4:15. This precious truth, received and dwelling in the conscience by the power of the Spirit, inspires the heart with heavenly love, animates the soul with joyful hope, and influences the life to all holy obedience. We have known by the word of truth, and believed by the power of the Spirit, the love that God hath to us. 1 JOHN 4:16. Bless the Lord, O my soul. PSALM 103:1.

Most solemn reflection. Many a good profession of Christ has ended in an awful desertion from him. Jesus foresaw this, and therefore says, He who endures to the end, the same shall be saved. MARK 13:13. Who shall thus endure? Even he who can endure to be hated of all men for Christ's sake. Who then shall stand?

How shall we endure? By fearing lest we fall away; being confident we shall do so, unless the Lord strengthen us by his might, and keep us by his power. And therefore, daily looking to Christ, constantly feeding on him, and continually crying to him, we derive strength from him, that we may not draw back unto perdition, but believe to the saving of our souls. HEBREWS 10:39. Happy is the man who thus feareth always: but he that hardeneth his heart shall fall into mischief. PROVERBS 28:14.

We are saved from first to last wholly by grace, or the free favor of God. Good works do not entitle us to, nor keep us in the favor of God; yet if we obey not God's will in his word, we cannot enjoy the comforts of his love in his Son. Jesus gave himself for us, to purify us unto himself, a peculiar people, zealous of good works. TITUS 2:14. And God gives the Holy Ghost to them who OBEY him. ACTS 5:32.

Christ took on him our nature. Through the knowledge of Christ we are made partakers of the divine nature. 2 PETER 1:3, 4. He became one in flesh with us sinners, that we might be one with God in him. JOHN 17:21. He who knows and believes this love, dwelleth in God, and God in him. 1 JOHN 4:16. He who believeth hath the witness in himself. 1 JOHN 5:10.

Every believer may say, I am crucified with Christ. GALATIANS 2:20. For as Christ took on him my nature, and bore my sins in his own body on the tree, 1 PETER 2:24, so have I been baptized into Christ, and have put on Christ, in the power of the Spirit through faith. GALATIANS 3:27. Oh most precious life, to live by the faith of the Son of

God, in love, out of nature, above sin, beyond Satan, in a heaven of peace and joy! Lord, increase this life in me.

If Christ dwells in the heart by faith, that heart will dwell on Christ with love, aspire after Christ in hope, wait on him by diligence, and never rest satisfied till Christ's prayer is answered upon him, and he is with Christ, and beholds his glory. JOHN 17:24. O may this be my soul's daily experience!

Each night we go to rest should remind us of being laid in the dust; that sleep is the image of death, and our rising in the morning, of our resurrection to die no more; that we may die daily to sin, rise to righteousness, walk in newness of life, and set our affections on things above, where Christ liveth at the right hand of God. COLOSSIANS 3:1. What is your life? JAMES 4:14.

Where your treasure is, there will your heart be also. MATTHEW 6:21. Lord, who hast said this, search my heart, drive every rival thence: attract it wholly to thyself; dwell in it by faith. Possessing the unsearchable riches of Christ, we give up the vanities of earth for the substance of heaven, saying, Thou art my portion, O Lord. PSALM 119:57.

That heart which never saw its own desperate wickedness, will lightly esteem or totally reject Christ's righteousness. Oh may I be found in Christ, not having on my own righteousness. PHILIPPIANS 3:9.

Head-knowledge puffeth up with pride. The knowledge of the heart humbleth the soul. Then Christ is precious, free grace is glorious, holiness lovely, and sin exceeding sinful. O my soul, be clothed with humility. 1 PETER 5:5.

Established Christians have a clearer sight of their

corruptions within them, than of the gifts and graces of the Spirit bestowed on them: hence, they are found mourning over the former, and lamenting their want of more of the latter; ever praying to be found in JESUS, rejoicing to be accepted in the beloved Son of God, in whom is all their perfection, and upon whom they set their affections. COLOSSIANS 3:2.

Instead of fearing to die, why should I not daily and ardently long for death? For he is my Lord's messenger of peace, sent to summon me from a world of sorrow and woe, and from a body of sin and death, to be ever present with my Lord, who is my path of life, in whose presence is fullness of joy, and at whose right hand there are pleasures for evermore. He who hath wrought us for this selfsame thing is God, who also hath given unto us the earnest of the Spirit. 2 CORINTHIANS 5:5.

Instead of my inbred lusts and indwelling corruptions keeping me from Christ, they should urge me with more eager speed to him, for his grace to support me under them, and to subdue them under me. For he saith, All things are possible to him who believeth. MARK 9:23.

My salvation stands upon the truth of God, and the work of his beloved Son. As I have come to Christ upon his own invitation, it is impossible I should meet with rejection from him. For Christ is God, and it is impossible for God to lie. Begone then, cursed unbelief, which rejects the truth of God, and makes the God of truth a liar. Hear and obey thy Lord: Abide in me. JOHN 15:4.

One of the sweetest and shortest chapters in the Bible is Isaiah 12. All the blessings of time, and all the glories of eternity, are comprised in those words, "GOD IS MY SALVATION." *Behold* it as the greatest wonder. *Receive* it as the greatest truth. *Believe* it as the greatest joy. What then?

O then, says my soul, I shall at once get rid of all my fears: for "I WILL TRUST, AND NOT BE AFRAID." A peaceful conscience, a happy heart, a holy life, and a joyful prospect through death, all spring from faith in a once-despised and crucified Savior, but now risen and glorified Lord. Here is work for the constant meditation of thy heart and the hope of thy soul. Here is an object who demands, and is worthy of all thy affection. My meditation of him shall be sweet; I will be glad in the Lord. PSALM 104:34.

That soul who is not constantly watching will surely be smarting, or what is worse, will fall into dangerous sleeping. Slothfulness casteth into a deep sleep, and idle souls shall suffer hunger. PROVERBS 19:15. Awake to righteousness, and sin not. 1 CORINTHIANS 15:34. It is high time to awake out of sleep; for now is our salvation nearer than when we believed. ROMANS 13:11.

If we walk uncomfortably, we should humble and chide ourselves frequently for not believing God's word more steadily, obeying his commands more cheerfully, and trusting his promises more cordially. For shame, ye children of God, and members of Christ, let not your hearts be remiss in believing, your hands hang down in praying, nor your feet grow weary in walking in the ways of the Lord. Look up and see your Savior near, to quicken you now, and to receive you to himself soon. Consider, the Lord is at hand. PHILIPPIANS 4:5.

"God hath made us accepted in the Beloved," therefore he will never reject us as hated, because our acceptance is from nothing in ourselves; but to the praise of the glory of his grace. EPHESIANS 1:6. God will lose none of the revenue of the praise of the glory of his grace, therefore we shall not be lost; for where grace reigns, sin cannot rule, the law condemn, nor Satan destroy. O for more grace, to give more praise and more glory to the GOD OF ALL GRACE,

who hath called us unto his eternal glory by Jesus Christ.
1 Peter 5:10.

What am I now thinking of? This world? It passeth away. I
shall soon quit it, and see it in flames. Lord, save me from
its bewitching vanities. Of riches? They certainly make
themselves wings and fly away. Proverbs 23:5. If I possessed them, I could not hold them; the stiff hand of death
would soon make me let them go. O for the unsearchable
riches of Christ. Ephesians 3:8. Am I thinking of happiness? It has forsaken the earth. It is only to be found in
God's presence, where is fullness of joy, and at his right
hand, where there are pleasures for evermore. Psalm
16:11. How to strive against sin, exercise grace, resist
Satan, and perform my duty to my Lord's glory? Not that
we are sufficient of ourselves to think any thing as of ourselves, but our sufficiency is of God. 2 Corinthians 3:5. I
can do all things through Christ, who strengtheneth me.
Philippians 4:13.

Daily eye the Lord's holy law as thy rule of life. Look to
his beloved Son as thy life itself. Though thou canst not
live by the law, nor get life from the law, yet looking to
Jesus, and living on him, who fulfilled the law for us, thou
wilt walk according to the law. Lord, give me more of thy
life and thy love, that we may more delight in thy law
after the inward man. Romans 7:22.

When we behold the face of Christ by faith with joy, we see
our sins with sorrow, look back with shame and look forward in hope. The Christian's motto is, As sorrowful in himself, yet always rejoicing in the Lord. 2 Corinthians 6:10.

It is not right with the soul if it be not looking to Jesus
to be saved from all sin, as well as to be justified from all
condemnation for sin. Both from the power, as well as the
guilt of sin, Good Lord, deliver me.

"Our conversation," rather citizenship, "is in heaven." PHILIPPIANS 3:20. We have a full right and clear title in Christ to all the privileges and immunities, blessings and enjoyments of this glorious city. The chief captain told Paul, With a great sum obtained I the freedom of Rome; but, says Paul, I was free born. ACTS 22:28. So the Son of God makes us free without money and without price. We are free born by his Spirit into the city of heaven. Is it so? Then let us solace ourselves in the rich charter of our Father's everlasting love, our Savior's everlasting salvation, and pray to the blessed Spirit to fill us with everlasting consolation. Looking for the appearing of Jesus Christ, the great God, and our Savior. TITUS 2:13.

Whither am I going? The way of all flesh. To the grave as fast as the swift wings of time can carry me. Is it for me then to follow the pleasures of the world, and the joys of sense? No. To whom should a poor dying sinner go, but to thee, O Savior? For thou hast the words of eternal life. JOHN 6:68. Thou sayest, "COME UNTO ME." MATTHEW 11:28. May thy precious invitation ever sound in my ears, and encourage my heart.

What am I now listening to? Satan's suggestions? These rob my Lord of his glory, and my soul of his love. Satan's accusations? These rob my Lord of his truth, and my soul of his peace. Satan's solicitations? These, if yielded to, will wound my soul, grieve the Spirit, and cause my Lord to hide away his face. Therefore I will hear what God the Lord will speak. He will speak peace. O suffer me not to turn again to folly. PSALM 85:8.

Hast thou, O my soul, lost thy sense of peace? Yet that faithful word abideth for ever, Christ is our peace. EPHESIANS 2:14. He hath made peace through the blood of his cross. COLOSSIANS 1:20. Receive this truth. Honor it. Cleave to it. Hang upon it. Reject peace from every

other quarter. For this adds boldness to faith, encouragement to hope, strength to patience, life to duty, quicken-
ing to prayer, excitement to look and wait for the times
of refreshing which shall come from the presence of the
Lord. ACTS 3:19.

A saint cannot continue in sin, because grace abounds.
Though sin does continue in him as a fallen creature, yet
the grace of God ever abounds to him, as a new creature
in Christ Jesus. Walk in the Spirit, and ye shall not fulfil
the lusts of the flesh. GALATIANS 5:16.

If sin had not killed God's Son on earth, it would for ever
have damned every son of man to hell. The death of Christ
is the life of our souls, and the death of our sins. Do we
really believe this? Then we shall most assuredly love
Jesus, who hath saved us by his death; and hate our sins,
which crucified him, and would for ever have damned our
souls. Faith worketh by love. GALATIANS 5:6.

We get strange unscriptural notions of inherent grace,
and of inherent righteousness. These only puzzle our
heads, perplex our hearts, puff up our spirits with pride,
and obscure to our souls the rich grace or free favor of
our Lord Jesus Christ in dying for the sins and to save
the souls of us poor sinners. Such notions also blind our
eyes to his everlasting righteousness, in which we are
perfectly complete and for ever justified. Christian experience of grace in the heart is by the Spirit's enlighten-
ing our understanding to see Christ, who is our hope,
1 TIMOTHY 1:1; taking of the things of Christ, and showing
them to us, thereby filling us with all joy and peace in
believing, that we may abound in hope, by the power of
the Holy Ghost, ROMANS 15:13; and so glorifying Christ to
our hearts, as our life, our righteousness, our sanctification, and our salvation, that we finding and feeling our
own emptiness, vileness, misery, poverty, and nakedness,

might live upon his fullness, and be continually receiving from him grace for grace, favor upon favor. Thus we are humbled and Christ exalted. Therefore be strong in the grace or favor of our Lord Jesus Christ. 2 TIMOTHY 2:1.

There is most danger of falling where there is the greatest self-confidence of standing. Peter was on the brink of a terrible fall when all within was secure and self-confident. He was left to his free-will pride and self-confident power. Lo, he fell. Thou standest by faith—of God's power: be not high-minded, but fear. ROMANS 11:20. Fear falling constantly. Be crying continually, Hold thou me up, and I shall be safe. PSALM 119:117.

Though I cannot always say, in full assurance of faith, Christ loved *me*, and gave himself for *me;* yet I may always, in the fullest assurance of faith, say, Christ loved sinners, and gave himself for sinners. For this is a faithful saying, and worthy of all acceptation, that Christ Jesus came into the world to save sinners. 1 TIMOTHY 1:15. O my soul, receive, honor, and live upon this truth by faith, and the Spirit will give thee the comfort of assurance from it; for he who hath received his testimony, hath set to his seal that God is true. JOHN 3:33.

"Away with all head notions of the doctrines of the gospel," say some. Lord, grant that they may sink down into my heart, say I; for as food must be received into the mouth, and be digested in the stomach before it can nourish the body, so the words of faith and of good doctrine must be received into the understanding and digested in the judgment before they can be experienced in the heart, and become nourishing to the soul. Brethren, be not children in understanding, but in understanding be ye men. I CORINTHIANS 14:20. Let Paul's prayer for Timothy be ours: The Lord give us understanding in all things. 2 TIMOTHY 2:7.

To follow Christ in the safe and narrow path of regeneration, is to avoid the equally dangerous broad road of proud legality on the right, and licentious antinomianism on the left. Every way of a man is right in his own eyes. PROVERBS 21:2. Search me, O God, and see if there be any wicked way in me, and lead me in the way everlasting. PSALM 139:23, 24.

Peter had lost sight of his precious Lord's love, or he had never been so frightened at the voice of a weak damsel. But loving Jesus never lost sight of unloving Peter. One look of Christ broke Peter's heart for his sins, melted it into sorrow for his fall, and brought him back to his Lord with shame. Mourn, O my soul, for thy sins. Praise thy Lord that his love is everlasting. Rejoice in him; his long-suffering is thy salvation. 2 PETER 3:15.

Satan, the enemy of all truth, preaches the doctrine of God's election, for despair and damnation to poor sinners, and to prevent their coming to Christ for salvation. The Spirit of truth shows them Christ's free promises and hearty invitations to come unto him. God's secret purposes in eternity are not contrary to his word in time by his Son. And he saith, This is the will of the Father, that every one who seeth the Son, and believeth on him, may have everlasting life. JOHN 6:40. I charge thee, O my soul, take courage from the warrant of God's word by Christ, so shalt thou find the comfort of his electing love in Christ. Secret things belong unto the Lord our God; let us not pry into them: but those things which are revealed belong unto us and our children for ever. DEUTERONOMY 29:29. Search the Scriptures; they testify of Christ, and salvation by him. JOHN 5:39.

Paul says, I do not frustrate the grace of God. GALATIANS 2:21. Take heed you do not. Many do. Beware lest, by any means, you frustrate or make void the grace of God

respecting your soul. The grace of God is his free favor
to the sinful, lost, guilt-cursed sinners of mankind. This
free favor is manifested in Christ his beloved Son. Hence
it is we are so called upon by God's word to believe in his
Son Christ Jesus. For there is no favor of God to us out of
Christ. But all grace or favor abounds to us in him. Yea,
where sin abounded, grace did much more abound. For
though sin hath reigned unto death, yet grace, or the free
favor of God, REIGNS over man's sin, over man's deserved
wrath, over the self-righteous pride of his nature, over
the rebellion of his will, over the enmity of his mind, over
the carnality of his affections, yea, over all that is in him
that opposes God, and all the curses of the law which are
against him. Therefore do not frustrate this glorious grace
in your own conscience by thinking it reigns because of
any inherent righteousness or goodness of yours. This will
instantly make it void and of no effect to your peace, comfort, and joy. For sin hath reigned unto death in you; but
grace reigns through the righteousness of Jesus Christ
unto eternal life. ROMANS 5:21. For if righteousness came
by the law, by any work of obedience of ours, then Christ
lived and died in vain. Grace is frustrated, and your
faith is made void, and the promise made of none effect.
Romans 4:14.

Take heed to yourselves, saith our Lord. LUKE 17:3. Save
yourselves, saith St. Peter. ACTS 2:40. Look to yourselves,
saith St. John. 2 JOHN 8. Keep yourselves, saith St. Jude.
JUDE 21. This salutary advice is liable to be turned into
poison by the spirit of pride and legality which works in
us. As though our Lord had not fully atoned for our sins,
perfectly justified us in his righteousness, clearly entitled
us to God's favor and kingdom, and finished salvation for
us; but had left us some part of this to do for ourselves.
This is directly contrary to our precious faith in Christ. So
it is liable also to be abused by the spirit of sloth and licentiousness which works in us. As though, because Christ is

our atonement, righteousness, sanctification, and salvation, therefore we have nothing to do with the directions
and exhortations of his word and Spirit to obey them. This
is quite opposite to our love to Christ, and hope in him.
Beware of each of these extremes. Let no man deceive us
with vain words. For it is our bounden duty, and we are
called to unremitting diligence in it, to obey the word of
Christ, and the Spirit of Christ in the word; to abstain
from the very appearance of evil; to cleave to that which
is good; to take heed to ourselves, lest our faith be weak-
ened, our love be wounded, and the Holy Spirit grieved;
to save ourselves from the corrupt principles and sinful
practices of this wicked world; to look to ourselves, and
consider our walk and way; to keep ourselves, by the love
and favor of God, diligently studying, and conscientiously
following those things which please him and make for our
peace; and in which we shall enjoy the sense of God's love
in our hearts, and sweet fellowship with him in our spirits:
For if ye do these things, ye shall never fall. 2 PETER 1:10.

Do we fear and tremble at the sight of our own superla-
tively deceitful and desperately wicked hearts? Let us fear
and tremble also lest we should either be left to ourselves,
to trust in ourselves, to have any confidence in what we
are utterly destitute of, a righteousness of our own. For
saith the Lord, Cursed be the man that trusteth in man.
JEREMIAH 17:5. Or be left to ourselves, so that inbred lusts
bring forth outward sins, to the death of our peace, hope,
and comfort, and to the destruction of our souls. Sinful,
hopeless, and desperate as our state is, and as we see it to
be, yet that precious word is ever sufficient to relieve us.
Blessed is the man that trusteth in the LORD, and whose
hope the LORD is. JEREMIAH 17:7. Oh the joy of this word
from the Holy Ghost to poor sinners: "CHRIST IN YOU, THE
HOPE OF GLORY." COLOSSIANS 1:27.

Every believer in Christ was given by the Father to

Christ, is a disciple of Christ, is prayed for by Christ, and shall most assuredly be with Christ where he is, to behold his glory. JOHN 17:24. But who is such a believer, such a disciple, who shall be thus glorified? This is the turning point. He that believeth hath the witness in himself. 1 JOHN 5:10. He has the inward evidence that Jesus is the Son of God. His heart and conscience are divinely assured of it through faith. And hereby we do know that we know him, if we keep his commandments. 1 JOHN 2:3. Also the Spirit itself beareth witness with our spirits, that we are the children of God. ROMANS 8:16. And to crown all, our Lord has fully assured us, that he who endureth to the end, in humble faith, holy love, and sincere obedience, the same, in spite of all the powers of earth and hell, shall be saved. MARK 13:13.

Many complain of their doubts and fears concerning their state in Christ, and their hope of eternal salvation by Christ. Better to be exercised with holy fear and godly jealousy over ourselves, than to fall into the sleep of vain confidence in ourselves. Woe to them who are at ease in Zion. AMOS 6:1.

What am I *now* looking at? my sins? Behold the Lamb of God, who taketh away the sin of the world. JOHN 1:29. The holy law and its dreadful curses? Behold "THE LORD OUR RIGHTEOUSNESS." JEREMIAH 23:6. He was made sin for us, that we might be made the righteousness of GOD IN HIM. 2 CORINTHIANS 5:21. Christ hath redeemed us from the curse of the law, being made a curse for us. GALATIANS 3:13. He hath fulfilled all its righteous precepts, and suffered all its dreadful penalties for us. Thus hath he magnified the law, and made it honorable. ISAIAH 42:21. At God's justice? Behold, God is just, and the justifier of him who believeth in Jesus. ROMANS 3:26. At the imperfections of my graces, and the short-comings of my best duties? Behold, God hath made us accepted in his beloved Son.

EPHESIANS 1:6. At the world? It is God's enemy, Satan's trap, and thy snare; for it lieth in wickedness. 1 JOHN 5:19. If any man love the world, the love of the Father is not in him. 1 JOHN 2:15. This is the victory that overcometh the world, even our faith. 1 JOHN 5:4. At death? Look to Christ, and sing victory over it. Thanks be unto God, who giveth us the victory through our Lord Jesus Christ. 1 CORINTHIANS 15:57. Lord, turn away mine eyes from beholding vanity. PSALM 119:37.

Believer, do you mourn that sin, the cause of all evils, dwells in you? Rejoice; for Christ is in you, the hope of glory. COLOSSIANS 1:27. This is the riches of the glory of God's mystery made known in the gospel, and enjoyed by faith; for Christ dwells in our hearts by faith. EPHESIANS 3:17. Do not you too often overlook this precious truth, this glorious hope? Quite opposite this, to all our natural, legal, self-righteous hopes. It was neither procured by our best works, nor prevented by our worst sins, from entering into our hearts. But this mysterious hope no sooner is possessed, but it counteracts the mystery of iniquity which works in us; for this is an eternal experimental truth: Every man who hath this hope in him, that is, in Christ, purifieth himself, even as he is pure. 1 JOHN 3:3. My Lord, my hope, may my soul constantly cleave to thee, and continually derive purity from thee.

Where was Paul's inherent stock of grace, rich experience, manifold gifts, rapturous joys, fine frames, and comfortable feelings, that these could not support him when Satan buffeted him? Ah no; even the inspired, highly favored, holy apostle Paul found himself just the very same poor, needy, helpless sinner as we are. He wanted what we do. He sought, as we ought, to none but the Lord in his distress. But even Paul knew not what to pray for any more than we; for he besought the Lord that the thorn in the flesh might depart from him. Christ knew it was better it should continue with him. Christ's answer was better than Paul's petition. He wanted ease from his distress. Christ says to him, under it, My grace is sufficient for thee; for my strength is made perfect in thy weakness. See, O my soul, what thou hast to look to: the free favor of Jesus. See what thou hast to rely on: the strength of Christ. Learn thou daily of Paul. Most gladly therefore will I rather glory—in what? My inherent grace, righteousness, perfection of strength? No, but—in my infirmities. Why? that the power of Christ may rest on me. 2 CORINTHIANS 12:9. Precious glorying! thus is self abased, Christ exalted, and Satan defeated. These things were written for our learning. ROMANS 15:4.

Hear the invariable decree of truth: ALL who will live godly in Christ Jesus shall suffer persecution. 2 TIMOTHY 3:12. Never think the world is grown better affected to the truths of Christ, or better humored with the godly in Christ. Do you escape persecution, at least that of the tongue, cruel mockings, for Christ? Are not you a byword of reproach, and nicknamed a Methodist, or some such name? No, says the decent professor, Christianity is more in fashion than it was; besides, I do not carry matters so far as many do. So you think to make the Spirit of truth a liar, by finding the art of living godly in Christ, without suffering persecution for Christ. Be assured, it is only an art to deceive your own soul. You are just as artful as that sick man who deceived the doctor by throwing away the medicines prescribed, instead of taking them; but he died for his folly. Do you beware.

Christ is the soul's health and salvation. A mere profession of him may get us a name to live when we are dead to the love of him. But this will neither cure our spiritual maladies, nor save our souls. Profess Christ we may, without fellowship with him, sanctification and comfort from him, living godly in him, and suffering persecution for him.

Possess him in the faith and love of our hearts, and hope
of our souls, we cannot, without denying ourselves daily,
taking up our cross constantly, and following him obedi-
ently. This is to be a disciple of Christ. Says our Lord, If
ye continue in my word, *then* are ye my disciples indeed.
JOHN 8:31. Hear his three negatives: He who hateth not his
own life, *cannot* be my disciple; Whosoever doth not bear
his cross and come after me, *cannot* be my disciple; He
who forsaketh not all that he hath, *cannot* be my disciple.
LUKE 14:33. Sit down and count the cost. By faith in our
Lord we receive his truths in love, and obey them in sin-
cerity. Through unbelief, professors find many ways so to
explain away Christ's meaning, that though a man loves
the world, is a friend of the world, and hath a good name
from the world, yet he may be a follower of Christ; and
therefore they make all our Lord's preaching only much
ado about nothing. Look to yourselves. 2 JOHN 8. If ye be
reproached for the name of Christ, happy are ye; for the
Spirit of glory and of God resteth upon you. 1 PETER 4:14.

All the sorrowings of hell can never make one soul sorry
for his sins against God, or one convert to the Son of God.
All the joys of heaven need not. The unconverted sinner
carries all the hell of enmity against God and Christ to
hell with him, and everlastingly retains it. The saint in
Christ carries the heaven of God's favor and Christ's love
to heaven with him, and for ever enjoys it. Heaven and
hell receive men just as they lived and died on the earth:
either in the faith of Christ and love to God, or in unbelief of Christ and hatred of God. As the tree falls, so it
lies. As death leaves us, judgment finds us, and heaven or
hell receives us. Behold, now is the accepted time. Beheld,
now is the day of salvation. 2 CORINTHIANS 6:2.

The terrors of the law may rack a natural man's conscience
with the dread of wrath, and fear of hell for sin, even
while he loves sin. The grace of the gospel, the good news

of the favor of God, and the love and salvation of Christ, break the believer's heart from sin, fill it with godly sorrow for sin, repentance, and hatred of sin, and godly hope of salvation, both from the power and being of all sin. The grace of God which bringeth salvation, teaches us to deny ungodliness, etc. TITUS 2:11, 12.

To pretend to believe the precious promises of salvation by Christ, and yet to walk contrary to the holy, self-denying commands of Christ, is only to mock Christ by profession, and deceive ourselves by a lie of Satan; for he who saith, I know Christ, and keepeth not his commandments, is a liar, and the truth is not in him; even now there are many antichrists. 1 JOHN 2:4, 18.

We walk by faith, and not by sight. 2 CORINTHIANS 5:7. We never saw the Son of God living upon the earth, dying on the cross, rising from the dead, and ascending up to heaven; yet we really believe in our hearts he did so. Why? because God hath told us this by the mouth of his chosen witnesses. ACTS 10:41. Yea, the Holy Ghost himself is a witness to us. HEBREWS 10:15. Not only so, but he who believeth on the Son of God, hath the witness in himself. 1 JOHN 5:10. He hath clear evidence and proof within himself that Christ is the Son of God, the Savior of sinners; for he finds his conscience relieved by what he believes of Christ, his heart attracted to Christ, his mind set on Christ, his affections going out after an unseen Christ, and he aims to walk so as to please Christ, who is the only object of his hope, for justification unto life. Thus it is clearly evident that Christ dwells in his heart by faith, and that he walks by the faith of invisible realities, though he is still the subject of corrupt nature, carnal reason, and sinful unbelief. These it is his folly ever to hearken to or consult. Against these it is his wisdom to fight the good fight of faith. 1 TIMOTHY 6:12.

Christian, here is thy Lord's word, yea, his note of hand offered thee: Verily, I say unto you, there is no man who shall suffer any loss for the kingdom of God's sake, who shall not receive manifold more in this life, and in the world to come life everlasting. LUKE 18:29, 30. Art thou guilty or not guilty of refusing to take thy Lord's word, and to credit his note? To trust a man's word, is to honor his veracity. To distrust his word and note, is the greatest indignity to him. Hast thou been afraid of suffering loss for thy Lord? Verily thou art guilty of this. An apothecary in the country, whose practice brought in upwards of five hundred pounds a year, was reduced to less than one hundred pounds by following Jesus. A lawyer of the same place, who was also a disciple of Christ, came to him and said, "What shall I do? I have got no clients." The apothecary replied, "And I have got no patients. I believe the Lord sees we should not make a right use of money, therefore he withholds it from us." Godliness, with contentment, is great gain. 1 TIMOTHY 6:6.

Many souls doubt of their election in Christ, who yet really choose Christ as their Beloved, cry to him as the Friend of sinners, trust in him for salvation, glory in him as their only hope, and desire to be found in him as their chief portion. Their doubt arises from that unbelief which works in their carnal nature; for Christ, the author of faith, does not totally kill our unbelief, but gives faith to resist its power, quell its risings, withstand its influence, and to look to him for victory. Thus he proportions our comfort: According to your faith be it unto you. MATTHEW 9:29. Give more diligence to make your calling and election sure. 2 PETER 1:10. So shall you enjoy the comfort of faith, and give Christ all the glory of it.

Many professors are blown up with strong, self-righteous confidence, who were never blown down by the wind of the Spirit's conviction. Hence, while God resisteth the proud, he giveth grace to the humble. JAMES 4:6. If you see your total vileness, and Christ's infinite preciousness, the Spirit hath, by the holy Scriptures, made you wise unto salvation, through faith which is in Christ Jesus. 2 TIMOTHY 3:15. Hallelujah, praise the Lord.

The belief of God's word is the foundation of hope, the source of comfort, and the spring of joy. It brings relief to the guilty, mercy to the miserable, pardon to the condemned, righteousness to sinners, justification to the ungodly, sanctification to the unholy, and the kingdom of heaven to hell-deserving men. For saith Christ, He that believeth on me hath everlasting life: this he confirms by his solemn oath, VERILY, VERILY. JOHN 6:47. Lord, open the Scriptures to me, and make my heart burn within me. LUKE 24:32.

False peace is easily obtained, eagerly embraced, and hardly parted with by us all; it is the devil's cradle, wherein he rocks us all asleep, and fills our heads with fine dreams of pleasing hopes. It is the strong man armed, who keeps the soul in fatal security, and at enmity against being at peace with God. How long? Till a stronger than he shall come upon him, overcome him, and take from him all his armor wherein he trusted. Who is this? The Man of God's right hand: whom he hath made strong for himself, PSALM 80:17, even the loving, powerful Jesus. Has he come upon you by the power of his truth? Has he overcome you by the strength of his love? Has he, by the sweetness of his grace, taken from you the armor of Satan's deceit wherein you trusted? And do you fall down at his cross as a love-conquered enemy, and bless him from your heart for having made peace by the blood of his cross? Hear, rejoice, love, and adore him; for he saith, No DOUBT the kingdom of God is come upon you. LUKE 11:20.

That sinner who, in the light of truth, has seen the glory

of Christ's precious person, the perfect obedience of his holy life, and his everlastingly finished salvation by his agonizing death on the cross, his mouth is stopped: he has done talking arrogantly, of fulfilling terms, and performing conditions of salvation. For the darkness is past, the true Light now shineth. 1 JOHN 2:8.

A miser well knows what it is to have fellowship in his heart with gold, which is his god. The man of pleasure finds fellowship in his affections with the delights of sense. The ambitions man feels in his mind the joy of fellowship with the honors of this world. Every natural man enjoys comfort from that object his heart is set on and his affections go after. Is the spiritual man, of all others, left destitute of the enjoyment of fellowship with his beloved object, God in Christ? Verily, if so, he is of all men most miserable. But, blessed be our gracious Lord, this is not our case. Though a mere formal professor may rest satisfied with the form and shadow of godliness, yet a real convert to Jesus finds the life, power, and substance of truth from Jesus, his living Head. From sweet heartfelt experience, he cries out with the beloved disciple, Truly our fellowship is with the Father, and with his Son Jesus Christ. 1 JOHN 1:3. And with David he says, Thou hast put gladness in my heart, more than in the time that carnal men have had the greatest increase of all their earthly enjoyments. PSALM 4:7.

Every carnal man well knows what will prevent his fellowship with, and interrupt his enjoyment of the particular idol his heart is set on, and that he studiously avoids. Whatever tends to increase his pleasure and heighten his joy in his idol, that he eagerly pursues. Oh Christian, shall the men of this world rise up against and condemn thee by their conduct in regard to earthly baubles? Shall they outstrip thee in wisdom and diligence? Art thou more remiss than they in pursuing heavenly and eternal

objects? What are all their enjoyments but vain, unsatis-
fying, and transitory? Are they to be compared with thy
objects, fellowship with God, the enjoyment of Christ in
the heart, the peace of God in your conscience, joy in the
Holy Ghost, and the prospect of heaven and eternal glory?
To convict us, and make us ashamed of our conduct, our
Lord says, The children of this world are, in their generation, wiser than the children of light. LUKE 16:8. It is high
time to awake out of sleep; for now is our salvation nearer
than when we first believed. ROMANS 13:11.

He who swims securely down the stream of self-righteous
confidence, is in danger of drowning in the whirlpool of
presumption. There is a generation that are pure in their
own eyes, and yet is not washed from their filthiness. Oh
how lofty are their eyes! and their eyelids are lifted up.
PROVERBS 30:12, 13.

In the sinless life of the Son of God we see what perfect
obedience the holy law requires from the sons of men for
their justification. In his agonizing death we behold what
wrath and curse are due to our sins, and what justice
demands as a satisfaction for sin; and without which no
sin could ever have been pardoned by a righteous God.
Hence faith cries out in ecstasy,

> In Christ complete I shine;
> His life, his death, are mine.

Take heed how you conceive and speak of David's com-
plicated sins; of Peter's lying, swearing, and denying
his Lord; or any of the saints' falls, so as to cause you
to think or speak lightly of sin, or to encourage you in
sin; as though God did not see sin, or does not hate sin,
but winks and connives at sin in his people. Be assured,
saints' falls left on record are not to make sin appear one
whit less exceedingly sinful to God or us, but to convince

us what sinful beings we all are. To strike our minds with a just sense of the evil and desert of sin, notice their bitter moans and complaints under a sense of guilt, the fears and terrors which haunted their souls for their sin; with the displays of God's love in Christ, in pardoning and restoring broken-hearted sinners, and the efficacy of the blood of Christ in cleansing them from all sin. 1 JOHN 1:7. If a king pardons a rebel, and restores a traitor to his favor, though this exalts the grace of majesty, yet it by no means extenuates the crimes of treason and rebellion. After Paul gives an awful account of the judgments of God against sin, he adds, Now all these things happened unto them for ensamples; and they are written for our admonition, etc. 1 CORINTHIANS 10:11. Stand in awe, and sin not. PSALM 4:4.

Here lies the essential difference between the Pharisee and the profane. In the latter, sin reigns outwardly: he obeys the flesh, and fulfils the lust thereof in his life. He is an open sepulchre. In the former, pride rules in the heart. In all he does he aims to get a good opinion of himself, and to recommend himself to God's favor and acceptance by his own works. He is a whitened sepulchre; he appears outwardly righteous unto men, but is inwardly abominable to God; for he rejects the truth of God, and submits not to the righteousness of the Son of God. Christian, you may see the true picture of your own nature in both. You have nothing whereof to glory over either. This is the true character of us all by nature. Stiff-necked, uncircumcised in heart, ye do always resist the Holy Ghost. ACTS 7:51. Lord, what is man, that thou art mindful of him? PSALM 8:4. O visit me with thy salvation. PSALM 106:4.

When Christians meet together, if Christ be not the end of their conversation, Satan will get advantage over them, and bring accusation against them; and their own hearts will condemn them. Be not ignorant of Satan's devices. Let your conversation be as it becometh the gospel of Christ. PHILIPPIANS 1:27. That you may be comforted together by your mutual faith. ROMANS 1:12.

Though a believer's salvation be not cast upon uncertain *ifs* and doubtful conditions, yet *if* any professor walk not in holy fellowship with Christ—*if* he follow not after holiness in the strength of Christ—*if* he be not striving against sin through the grace of Christ, he can have no evidence of his faith in Christ. He will soon fall away from professing Christ. For says our Lord, My sheep hear my voice, and follow me. JOHN 10:27.

Every sinner quickened by the Spirit of God is a living believer on the Son of God. He sees his vileness, feels his misery, and deplores his wretchedness. Am I one? If so, then I *was* an object of God's great love from eternity; I *am* a miracle of his sovereign grace now; and I *shall* be a trophy of his rich mercy in endless glory. I am a mystery to myself, the joy of holy angels, the scorn of carnal men, and the envy of infernal devils. But I am the glory of Christ, and my Christ is my glory. Glory be to thee, O Lord. By thy grace I am what I am. 1 CORINTHIANS 15:10.

Unbelief of God's word, of all sins is the most capital. It is the parent of every other sin. It credits the father of lies, and makes the God of truth a liar. 1 JOHN 5:10. We do not find even the very devils charged with it, for they believe. JAMES 2:19. But all unregenerate sinners live under the power of it. Yet they see not its evil, confess not its guilt, nor dread its consequence; though it leaves the soul without hope, seals it under wrath, and issues in damnation. For says Christ, If ye believe not that I am he, ye shall die in your sins. JOHN 8:24. He that believeth not, shall be damned. MARK 16:16. Have I obtained precious faith in the righteousness of God and our Savior Jesus Christ? 2 PETER 1:1. O may I love and rejoice in Christ the author, and serve him continually, who is the finisher of my faith. HEBREWS 12:2.

He who prays most in the Spirit, obeys least the motions of the flesh. Lord, help me to pray without ceasing. 1 THESSALONIANS 5:17.

Many complain for want of what they call the faith of assurance; while they neglect the word of truth, by which we are blessed with the full assurance of faith. HEBREWS 10:22. Is God's word truth or fiction, fact or fable? If we want more than that to assure our faith, to bring assurance to our hearts, and to cause us, in full assurance of faith, to draw nigh to God, we tempt God and grieve his Holy Spirit. Not from any thing we find and feel in ourselves, have we boldness to enter into the presence of God, but by the blood of Jesus; whereof the Holy Ghost is witness to us. HEBREWS 10:15, 19.

By a firm and steady belief of the truths of Jesus, we have a true heart, by the truth dwelling in it. By the belief of the truth, our hearts are sprinkled from a guilty conscience, we have peace with God, and devote ourselves to God. Mourning sinner, think not lightly of the truths of God's word. Look more to them for the comfort of the Spirit in belief of them. Hold fast the profession of faith without wavering, for faithful is He who hath promised. The truth shall make you free, JOHN 8:32—free from the guilt of sin, from legal fears and slavish doubts; free to run the ways of God's commands with delight; and in believing to rejoice with joy unspeakable and full of glory. 1 PETER 1:8. Believe the Spirit's witness in the word, and you shall enjoy his testimony in your heart.

That soul which grows most in the grace of God, grows most out of conceit with himself. The darkness is past, the true light now shineth. 1 JOHN 2:8.

 He who is married to Christ by faith, is divorced from his sins by the love of Christ, and dead to the law by the body of Christ. ROMANS 7:4.

He who believes that Christ shed his precious blood on the cross for the remission of sin, trusting in his righteousness for justification unto life, and looking unto Jesus as a Savior from all sin, having now received the atonement, has nothing to fear from the wrath revealed against sin, ROMANS 5:11, nor from the curse of the law for sin; for being in Christ, there is no condemnation against him, ROMANS 8:1, he is justified from all things, ACTS 13:39; nor from death, for he is fit for death, and meet for glory. Hence this is his daily duty, and is to be his constant work, to live a life of love and praise, giving thanks unto God the Father, who hath made us meet to be partakers of the inheritance of the saints in light. COLOSSIANS 1:12.

If we love sin, and live in sin, we are only baptized infidels. If we trust in our works, gifts, or graces, we are proud Pharisees. If we come to a throne of grace with, God be merciful to me a sinner, and to Christ's feet with, Lord, save, or I perish, we are humble Christians and holy saints, who rejoice in Christ Jesus, and have no confidence in the flesh. PHILIPPIANS 3:3. Though Christ by his own sacrifice hath entirely put away the guilt of our sins from before God, and by his own righteousness hath perfectly justified us from all condemnation of the law in the sight of God, still he leaves the old man of sin alive in us, perfect and entire in all his parts. Why so? For the exercise of our faith in him as our Priest; to try our submission to him as our Prophet; and to prove our allegiance to him as our King. The sight of the total corruption of our nature, and of the exceeding sinfulness of sin in us, humbles us to the dust before Christ, excites love and gratitude to him for his finished salvation of us, and causes us ever to glory in him, THE LORD OUR RIGHTEOUSNESS. JEREMIAH 33:16. And we give glory to him; for though sin dwells in us, yet sin shall not have dominion over us, for we are under his grace. ROMANS 6:14.

Were we to see perfection in ourselves, Narcissus-like, we should fall in love with our own beauty, pine away, and die in our folly. We should be blinded to the infinite charms of Christ, dead to the wonderful love of Christ, and not glory in the precious grace, spotless righteousness, and finished salvation of Christ. The constant sense of our imperfections causes us to take refuge in Christ, as suited to our desperate state, makes Christ infinitely glorious in our eyes, and inestimably precious to our hearts. For he saith, Their righteousness is of me. ISAIAH 54:17. Continue ye in my love. JOHN 15:9.

We faint when we should flee, crawl when we should run, halt when we should walk, turn back when we should press forward, droop when we should rejoice. Why? Because we look down, look within, look back, or to the right or left, when we should look steadfastly up to Jesus our forerunner, who is *for us* entered within the veil, HEBREWS 6:20, there to appear in the presence of God *for us*. HEBREWS 9:24. He has set an open door before us. REVELATION 3:8. He ever lives to save unto the uttermost. HEBREWS 7:25. He says, I will receive you to myself, that where I am, there ye may be also. JOHN 14:3. Now after all this, may he not justly upbraid each of us with, O fools, and slow of heart to believe all that is written concerning me? LUKE 24:25.

The Lord will ever be mindful of his covenant. PSALM 111:5. That is our comfort and security. But shame to us that we are so unmindful of the covenant love of Jehovah, which Father, Son, and Spirit entered into for us; of Jesus our covenant surety, who has fulfilled all covenant terms and conditions in our behalf; of covenant grace, from which all

present blessings are bestowed on us; of covenant faith-
fulness, by which future glory is insured to us; of covenant influences of the Holy Spirit, to lead and guide us
into all truth, to sanctify us through the truth, to comfort
us by the truth, and to glorify us according to the truth.
Lord, deeply impress our hearts with this truth, that we
may live more under the influence of it: All things are of
God, who hath reconciled us to himself by Jesus Christ.
2 CORINTHIANS 5:18.

Be ye perfect, even as your Father who is in heaven is
perfect. MATTHEW 5:48. This the eternal, immutable law
of God requires. Without this perfection no soul can be
saved. Where is it to be found? The everlasting gospel
reveals it. Behold this perfectly righteous character, fully
commensurate to the standard of all perfection, in the
man Christ Jesus. Look for it in any one besides, and you
will be deceived. What says faith to this? O that I may be
found IN HIM. PHILIPPIANS 3:9; and be presented perfect IN
Christ Jesus, COLOSSIANS 1:28; not having spot or wrin-
kle, or any such thing. EPHESIANS 5:27. Lord, humble me
under the ministration of condemnation, which was glorious. Lord, exalt me by the ministration of righteousness,
which exceeds in glory. 2 CORINTHIANS 3:9.

God glorifies us with his rich graces from heaven, that
we may glorify him in our lives and conversations on
earth, till he brings us to heaven. He says of all his justified ones, This people have I formed for myself; they shall
show forth my praise. ISAIAH 43:21.

Though as a believer you have put on Christ, for all the
purposes of pardon, justification, sanctification, and eternal life, yet remember you are to put him on afresh from
day to day, in your heart, memory, and conscience, for all
the purposes of comfort, love, and obedience. Lord, teach
me daily this heavenly art.

Let not your mournful complaints of what you find and what you feel in yourself banish thankfulness from your heart for what Jesus hath done for you, still is to you, and is in you the hope of glory. COLOSSIANS 1:27.

If you do not rejoice in the Lord alway, PHILIPPIANS 4:4, you disobey your Lord's precious command, dishonor his perfect work, and rob your soul of the comfort to which he hath called you, and for which he hath formed you.

Be it unto thee according to thy faith. This is thy Lord's rule of proportion as to peace and joy. If you believe that you have perfect remission of sins in his blood, perfect justification before God, a perfect title to glory in his righteousness, and are perfectly accepted in him THE BELOVED, your conscience will be at perfect peace with God, and you will continually joy in God, perfecting holiness in the fear of God. 2 CORINTHIANS 7:1.

If we are not diligent in the ways of God, we shall not be joyful in the comfortable promises of God. Be diligent, that ye may be found of him in peace. 2 PETER 3:14.

Though that moment we believe in Jesus we are freed from all condemnation, yet from that very moment we are bound by the strongest ties to universal obedience. The love of Christ constraineth us. 2 CORINTHIANS 5:14.

If we have not power over *all* sin, we walk not in the full liberty of the gospel, and enjoy not the complete victory of faith in Jesus. How shall we who are dead to sin, live any longer therein? ROMANS 6:2.

The prize of eternal life is sure to all who are in Christ Jesus. But we cannot be sure we are in Christ without humble believing, holy walking, constant praying, daily watching, continual striving against sin, and perfecting holiness in the fear of the Lord. 2 CORINTHIANS 7:1.

If we call evangelical obedience legal, we shall soon become licentious. Woe be to them that call good evil. ISAIAH 5:20.

Whenever thy soul feels the burden of sin, it is the work of faith and obedience to the truth instantly to cast thy burden upon the Lord; he will sustain thee. PSALM 55:22.

To trust to any thing in ourselves to entitle us to the favor of God and eternal life, is to please the father of lies, to give the lie to the God of truth, to deny the faith of Jesus, and to reject the witness of the Spirit. 1 JOHN 5:10.

When a Christian gives way to sinful passions, he dishonors his profession, grieves the Spirit of God, and makes sport for infernal spirits. Be not overcome of evil. ROMANS 12:21.

Every believer in Christ will reckon himself a poor sinner, because he daily finds and feels he really is such, and he hates hypocrisy. While the sense of his poverty humbles him, it drives him out of himself, and makes him look to the unsearchable riches of Christ. The knowledge of his sin makes Jesus the Savior precious to him. 1 PETER 2:7.

Every regenerate man believes in his heart unto righteousness, and is entitled to everlasting life; yet unbelief is in his nature, which works unto sin and death. But grace reigns through righteousness over him unto eternal life by Jesus Christ. ROMANS 5:21.

Though indwelling sin does not produce the grace of humility in a child of God, yet it beats down the natural pride of his heart, and makes him cry with Paul, O wretched man that I am! ROMANS 7:24.

Though the holy walk of a Christian does not recommend him to the favor of God, yet it recommends the religion of the Son of God in the world, and is an evidence that he is born of God. 1 JOHN 2:29.

Why does a Christian sorrow for his sins, when they are perfectly atoned for by the blood of Christ? Because he loves God his Father, and cannot forgive himself for sinning against the rich love and abundant grace of Jesus his Savior, and for grieving the Spirit his Comforter, by whom he is sealed unto the day of redemption. EPHESIANS 4:30.

No sinner ever went to heaven with one spot of sin upon his soul. The blood of Jesus Christ cleanseth from all sin. 1 JOHN 1:7. No sinner ever went to hell with one grain of the faith of Christ in his heart. For Christ puts his solemn oath to it: Verily, verily, he that believeth on me hath everlasting life. JOHN 6:47.

No man ever knows God till he believes in Christ the Son of God; for he hath declared him. JOHN 1:18.

A god out of Christ is the idol of an infidel. God in Christ is the Christian's God. 2 CORINTHIANS 5:19.

He who wilfully sins today, shall woefully smart for it tomorrow. Even the loving Savior says, Except ye repent, ye shall perish. LUKE 13:3.

That heart which smarts not for sin on earth, will eternally suffer for it in hell. Godly sorrow worketh repentance unto salvation, not to be repented of. 2 CORINTHIANS 7:10.

Seeing God perfectly hates all sin, and as all his children also abhor sin, why does he suffer indwelling sin to remain in them? Because God prefers a humble sinner to a proud Pharisee. LUKE 18:14.

Never lose sight of this, Christ is our life. COLOSSIANS 3:4. He who believeth on him, is passed from death to life. JOHN 5:24. Though for a season the graces of faith, hope, love, etc., may appear to be totally extinct, and the soul dead; just as the trees in winter, wanting the sun's influence, the sap falls down to the root, and the life of vegetation appears not; or like a person stunned by a blow, or seized with a fit, the functions of life are suspended; so it may be with Christ's people. Yet he says, They shall never die. JOHN 11:26. The life of our souls is not in our own keeping: this is our mercy. The life of our graces is not in ourselves: this is our comfort. Christ is the life, both of our souls and our graces: this is our joy. For he says, Because I live, ye—all my members—shall live also. JOHN 14:19. This is our triumph. Learn daily to oppose Christ's truths to Satan's lies.

God loves his children too well, and hates sin too much, not to chastise them for sin, and whip them from sin. He is not that unwise father who spares the rod and spoils the child. Though Christ hath put away sin by the sacrifice of himself, yet if we are God's children, and brethren of Christ, he will surely make us sick of sin, and hate sin so as to depart from all iniquity, 2 TIMOTHY 2:19, and to delight to serve God in holiness and righteousness all the days of our life. LUKE 1:75.

Be angry, and sin not. EPHESIANS 4: 26. Be angry at sin, but not with the sinner. Take the three following instances: To be angry with one because he feels not his need of Christ's atonement for the pardon of his sins, is just as wise as to be angry with a dead corpse for not feeling its want of life. To be angry with a professor for not seeing his want of the righteousness of Christ, to be imputed to him for justification unto life, is just as foolish as to be angry with a blind man for not seeing that he is naked. Go and bless your Lord for opening your eyes to see the want of it, and

your heart to receive it by faith, and to enjoy the comfort
of it; when he shall be converted to the Lord, the veil shall
be taken off his heart. 2 CORINTHIANS 3:16. To be angry
with any one for denying the essential Godhead of Christ,
is just as absurd as to be angry with a child because it
cannot read when it does not know letters. For some are
ever learning, and never able to come to the knowledge of
Jesus, who is THE TRUTH. 2 TIMOTHY 3:7. Pity, Lord, their
ignorance. Jesus, increase my knowledge of thee, and
faith in thee, as my Lord and my God.

The flesh profiteth nothing, saith Christ. JOHN 6:63. In
our flesh dwells no good thing, saith St. Paul. ROMANS
7:18. Though we are not in the flesh, but in the Spirit, yet
how prone are we to look for power from ourselves, and
expect to find goodness in ourselves. And how does disap-
pointment bring on dejection! This is the foolishness of
folly. What, know ye not your own selves, how that Jesus
Christ is in you? 2 CORINTHIANS 13:5. And that the body
is dead because of sin? ROMANS 8:10. Divine Comforter,
teach me ever to glory in this thy truth: In the Lord have
I righteousness and strength. ISAIAH 45:24.

The one and only way to enjoy the comfort of God's love
in the heart, is to enter his open door, which is Christ, by
faith. Christ is the way and the door, JOHN 14:6; 10:9—the
way to God's heart of love, and the door to his kingdom of
glory. All God's promises are in him. 2 CORINTHIANS 1:20.
All the delight of God's soul is fixed on him. ISAIAH 42:1.
Yea, God himself is in Christ reconciled to sinners, not
imputing their trespasses unto them, 2 CORINTHIANS 5:18,
but bestowing his peace upon them. ROMANS 5:1. Study this
mystery of faith till you are lost in wonder, love, and praise.

Young Christians are apt to live too much on their sweet
frames and fine feelings; but as they grow in the grace
of God, and in the knowledge of Christ, they walk more

steadily by faith in God's everlasting love to them, and Christ's everlasting salvation of them, though not less prizing the sensible comforts of the Holy Ghost within them. But when these are withheld from them, still God in Christ is all in all to them; and his blessed word the glory of them. Therefore they obey his loving voice. When they walk in darkness and have no light, they trust in the name of the Lord, and stay themselves upon their God. ISAIAH 50:10. It is the glory of faith to honor God's word in the dark, to trust him when we have no light, and to stay our souls on him till the light of joy cometh from him. For says an old experienced saint, Weeping may endure for a night, but joy cometh in the morning. PSALM 30:5.

The kingdom of heaven is in every Christian's heart; for Christ the King of saints dwells there by faith. EPHESIANS 3:17. Yea, he dwells in Christ, and Christ in him. JOHN 6:56. He is passed from the kingdom of nature, death, and sin into the kingdom of grace, life, and righteousness. He enjoys heaven upon earth, and carries heaven in his soul to the kingdom of heaven in glory. Do you find it thus? Then take this blessed advice: Wherefore we receiving a kingdom which cannot be moved, let us have—hold fast—grace, the free favor of God in Christ, whereby we may serve God acceptably, with reverence and godly fear; for OUR God is a consuming fire, HEBREWS 12:28, 29, to all who despise his grace in Christ, serve him not with reverence, and are destitute of godly fear. What hast thou that thou didst not receive? 1 CORINTHIANS 4:7. As ye have received Christ, so walk ye in him. COLOSSIANS 2:6.

Vile and vain thoughts are the Christian's burden and guilt. To entertain them is his fault and his shame. To cast them out of his mind, as unwelcome and intruding guests, is his wisdom and glory; and to invite his Lord is his constant duty: for he hath said, I will dwell in them, and walk in them. 2 CORINTHIANS 6:16.

If we go to prayer without Christ in the arms of our faith, we fancy we are rich in ourselves, and God will surely send us empty away. LUKE 1:53.

Mourning over deadness in duty is a sure proof that Christ is the life of the soul; especially when it complains to him, My soul cleaveth unto the dust, and cries, Quicken thou me according to thy word. PSALM 119:25.

We should daily strive and fervently pray to be warm-hearted soldiers of Christ, loving-hearted saints in him, and obedient-hearted disciples to him: ever gratefully asking, What shall I render unto the Lord for all his benefits towards me? PSALM 116:12.

These are genuine marks of a gracious soul, to love to talk of, to joy to hear of, and to delight to obey our precious Savior; and the more he speaks of him, and acts for his glory, the more he is humbled before God, sees in all he does that he is an unprofitable servant of God, and continually seeks pardon through the blood of and acceptance in the Son of God. Lord, strengthen me to work for thy glory, and ever keep me humble at thy feet.

"ABOUT YOUR BUSINESS," is the motto of a sun-dial. Obey this command. Christian, it is your chief business to put on the Lord Jesus Christ, and to put off the old man with his deceitful lusts. ROMANS 13:14; EPHESIANS 4:22.

If iniquity be regarded in the heart, the love of Christ will not prevail in the soul, nor the peace of God and the joy of faith in the conscience. Whatsoever a man soweth, that shall he also reap. GALATIANS 6:7.

Dark and uncomfortable frames of soul proceed from the strong corruptions of the flesh, and the great weakness of faith. Nothing but the light of God's truth, the grace of his Spirit, and the power of faith can expel them. Most precious promise from our covenant God: Unto you who fear my name shall the Son of righteousness arise, with healing in his beams. MALACHI 4:2.

All our comforts flow from the doctrines of God's favor to us in Christ. But they can only be enjoyed while our souls are under the transforming influence of that grace and truth which came by Jesus Christ, and is revealed in the word of grace and truth by the Spirit of Christ. For he hath saved us by the renewing of the Holy Ghost. TITUS 3:5.

Those short-lived pleasures which are reaped by sin are sure to be lost by after sorrow. What fruit had ye in those things whereof ye are now ashamed? For the end of those things is death, ROMANS 6:21—death to our present comfort, and death to our immortal souls. My Lord, I would eternally bless thee for saving me from living in them, and dying by them. For those who live in pleasure are dead while they live. 1 TIMOTHY 5:6.

Complaints of unbelief evidence the strugglings of faith in the heart. Canst thou appeal, Lord, I believe? With every believer on earth thou hast reason to add, Help thou my unbelief. MARK 9:24.

Groaning under corruptions before the Lord is a blessed sign of a sanctified spirit from the Lord; for he says, Blessed are they that mourn; for they shall be comforted. MATTHEW 5:4.

Glorious challenge of faith. Who shall lay any thing to the charge of God's elect? ROMANS 8:33. Not God the Father; for he chose them; he justifies them; his justice pardons them; his law is fulfilled for them; his truth is magnified in and by them; his mercy embraces them; his love is everlastingly fixed on them. God the Son will not; for he has fully discharged all dues, debts, and demands against them. God the Spirit will not; for he is the Comforter of them, witnesses of the Savior to them, and the fullness of his salvation for them. Who will? Satan, the accuser of the brethren of Christ. REVELATION 12:10. But says our Judge, He is a liar. JOHN 8:44. His evidence will not be heard in court. Then, O my soul, honor thy Lord's grace and truth; resist Satan steadfastly, in the faith of thy full and free justification before God in Christ. Ever glory also: there is no separation from the love of God which is in Christ Jesus. ROMANS 8:39.

Faith begets hope, and worketh by love. Fear is a fruit of faith, united to hope, and a companion of love. By these graces of the Spirit in the heart, the conscience is kept tender, the mind happy, and the life holy. Though these are no part of our justification before God, yet they are sure evidences that we are justified by the Son of God, and shall be ever with the Lord. 1 THESSALONIANS 4:17.

Does death knock at my door? Is he giving daily warnings? Must I soon fall by his dart? How sweet daily to familiarize death as my friend, and to admit him to my meditations as my companion, while I look at the life and death of my Savior; for he hath taken away the sting of death, which is sin. 1 CORINTHIANS 15:56. He hath reconciled me to God by the blood of his cross. COLOSSIANS 1:20. Therefore, with all our other blessings, death is ours also. 1 CORINTHIANS 3:22.

God is love, 1 JOHN 4:16; full of love: nothing but love to his children in Christ. He tells them, I have loved thee with an everlasting love. JEREMIAH 31:3. With everlasting kindness will I have mercy on thee. ISAIAH 54:8. Therefore he sees no sin in them for which he will ever hate them and eternally condemn them; for he is at peace with them, reconciled to them, and hath made them accepted in his beloved Son. EPHESIANS 1:6. His blood cleanseth them from all sin. 1 JOHN 1:7. His righteousness justifieth them from all condemnation. ROMANS 8:1. Nothing shall be able to separate them from the love of God in Christ. ROMANS 8:39. And they are kept by the power of God, through faith unto salvation. 1 PETER 1:5. "Fine licentious doctrine; then we may live as we list," say some. Thy speech betrays a proud, licentious heart, which has not been conquered by grace, received the truth in love, nor felt its holy influence. To such, God's words are the savor of death unto death. 2 CORINTHIANS 2:16. But says another, "I will live and die by this doctrine: it affords such ample provision for one's comfort and safety, and delivers us from all fear of falling away. Sin we ever so foully, yet we can never fall away finally." Thou hast strong words in thy mouth. Hast thou also strong faith in, strong love to, and strong fear of the God of all comfort in thy heart? True, it is an eternal truth, that the foundation of the Lord standeth sure, having this seal, The Lord knoweth them that are his. 2 TIMOTHY 2:19. But am I one? For it is also as true, the Lord sets a mark upon all who are his; they sigh and cry for the abominations of their nature. EZEKIEL 9:4. They are weary of their sins, and depart from iniquity. For their covenant LORD hath put his laws into their hearts, and in their minds he hath written them. HEBREWS 10:16. Yea, he hath put his *fear* into their hearts, that they shall not depart from him. JEREMIAH 32:40. For love is a fruit of faith; fear, an inseparable companion of faith and love. And true obedience to God springs from faith in his word, love to his glory, and fear of his name.

Do you delight in the law of God after the inward man? ROMANS 7:22. Do you fear to sin against God, to offend God, to depart from God? THEN in the fear of the Lord is strong confidence. PROVERBS 14:26. You have fellowship in the gospel, and may be confident of this very thing, that He who hath begun a good work in you, will perform it until the day of Jesus Christ. PHILIPPIANS 1:6. But ever fear to hold the truth in unrighteousness, knowing the wrath of God is revealed from heaven against all such. ROMANS 1:18. Ever remember, the Lord *thy* God is a jealous God. EXODUS 20:5. Yea, *our* God is a consuming fire. HEBREWS 12:29. Stand in awe, and sin not. PSALM 4:4. Therefore says every believer in Christ, Thy word have I hid in my heart, that I might not sin against thee. PSALM 119:11.

Carnal security most certainly possesses that heart whose carnal lusts are indulged in the life. The end of those things is death. ROMANS 6:21. Better to be miserable with a sense of sin, than to live securely under the power of sin. Grant, Lord, that the truth may make me free from all sin. JOHN 8:32.

Though there is no condemnation from God's holy law, and inviolable justice against any believer in Christ, ROMANS 8:1, yet he will surely feel condemnation and fear wrath, if he does not walk after the Spirit, live in and obey the truth, and judge of himself according to the truth as it is in Jesus. Lord, send out thy light and thy truth; let them lead me. PSALM 43:3.

He who feeds most upon Christ in his heart by faith, will have the least appetite for the vanities of time and the pleasures of sense. For Jesus saith, He who eateth me, even he shall live by me. JOHN 6:57. Ah, ye sons of sense and pleasure, ye despise us; we pity you. We have food to eat whose exquisite deliciousness ye know not. Lord, evermore give me this bread.

We are prone to look at our miseries through a magnifying glass, and at our mercies through a diminishing one. Hence we are so miserable under present distress, and so ungrateful for past favors. A small stream of trouble appears a torrent, a little brook of affliction a broad river, and a narrow river of distress the wide ocean. We remember not many years' health, so much as one day's sickness. The summer of our delights is too short; the winter of our afflictions too long. Impatience and ingratitude are bound up in the heart of man. O blessed, to say with Paul, I have learned in whatsoever state I am, therewith to be content. PHILIPPIANS 4:11. And in every thing giving thanks; for this is the will of God in Christ Jesus concerning you. 1 THESSALONIANS 5:18.

"All men think all men mortal but themselves." Death is thought on with reluctance, and submitted to with pain by those who know not Jesus, the conqueror of death. Death attacks one in the prime of life. He pleads that Death had given him no warning, and begs a respite to be prepared for him. Death retires, and promises to give him three warnings before he comes again. Lo, he comes in the winter of age. The man urges Death's breach of promise in not giving him the warnings, and that therefore he is not prepared. Death asks, How is your sight? The man replies, Very dim. Your hearing? Almost lost, says the man. Your strength? Alas, I am so feeble I can scarcely walk. Are not these three fair warnings? replies Death. The man is speechless, and dies without hope. Such fools men live and die. He who, being often reproved, hardeneth his neck, shall suddenly be destroyed, and that without remedy. PROVERBS 29:1. O believer, go and learn what thy Lord meaneth, that thou mayest enjoy all the comfort and blessedness of this truth, and triumph over death. Verily, verily, I say unto you, if a man keep my saying, he shall never see death. JOHN 8:51.

In nature's darkness we love and admire ourselves. In the light of truth, sight of the law, and view of Christ, we hate and abhor ourselves, love Christ, and become his followers; for he saith, If a man hate not his life, he cannot be my disciple. LUKE 14:26.

When Satan comes to you, do you go to Christ; when he tempts you to sin, do you try Christ's love, by crying to him with Hezekiah, O Lord, I am oppressed, undertake for me. ISAIAH 38:14.

Christians are ordained of God to walk in good works. EPHESIANS 2:10. But they abhor the thought of bribing God's justice by them, or trading with God for them, as though they were the price of his favor, and could purchase a title to his kingdom. This they have by the faith of Jesus only. Hence they have so learned Christ as to renounce all their works as filthy rags, and to count them as dross in point of justification before God; yet are careful to maintain the practice of them to justify their faith in Christ, and to manifest their love to God, for the honor of Christ, for the glory of God, and for the example and profit of their fellow-creatures and fellow-Christians. If we say we have fellowship with God, and walk in darkness, we lie, and do not the truth. 1 JOHN 1:6.

There is no dying to the world but by living with Jesus; no conquering the world, but by believing that he hath overcome it. JOHN 16:33. When Christ thus dwells in our hearts, we behold such glorious charms in him that the world is under our feet in contempt; for he says, Be of good cheer, I have overcome the world. JOHN 16:33. Lord, make thy conquest my triumph.

Profession of Christ without vital union to him by faith, may get us a name to live while we are dead. But those who live by faith on him, have communion with God, love to God, peace from God, joy in God. For Jesus is the only medium between God and us, and faith leads us, through his human nature, to the enjoyment of and fellowship with the Godhead. He who is joined unto the Lord is one spirit. 1 CORINTHIANS 6:17. Thus we are made perfect in one. JOHN 17:23. Hold fast this mystery of faith, so shalt them abound in love.

If we are not watchful, we cannot be joyful, but shall be woeful. Thou Captain of our salvation, speak thy word of command to our very souls, WATCH. MARK 13:37.

Did Satan dare to tempt the immaculate Son of God to the blackest of sins? Marvel not, though he tempts you, a fallen sinner, to the same. Satan's temptations are not your sins. Not you, but he shall answer for them. In and under all of them, remember the witness of the Holy Ghost for your tempted soul's comfort: we have a merciful High-priest, who is touched with a feeling of our infirmities, who was in all points tempted as we are. HEBREWS 4:15. Look unto him who feels for you in all, will succor you under all, and knows how to deliver you out of all. 2 PETER 2:9. Look less at your temptations, look more to your once tempted Jesus.

All experimental feelings by the teaching of the Spirit of truth are agreeable to the word of truth, and make Christ precious, who is THE TRUTH. Let the weak say, I am strong, saith the Spirit. JOEL 3:10. When I am weak, then I am strong, saith the experienced Christian. 2 CORINTHIANS 12:10. A heartfelt sense of our weakness causes us to go out of ourselves, not to consider ourselves, not to trust in ourselves, but to obey our Lord: Take hold of my strength. ISAIAH 27:5. Then out of weakness, in nature and self, we are made strong, HEBREWS 11:34—strong in the Lord, and in the power of his might, EPHESIANS 6:10; and cry out in the joy of faith, In the Lord, not in self, have I strength. ISAIAH 45:24. Thus to those who have no might in themselves, the Lord increases strength from himself. ISAIAH 40:29.

Lord, if I am not constantly hungering and thirsting for thee, I see not as I ought my want of thee; I am not as I ought alive to thee. O quicken my desires for thee, that my soul may continually feed on thee, who art the bread of life. JOHN 6:35.

Do we stand by faith? Then how safe, how holy, how happy is our standing! For faith receives the Lord Christ, and trusts in all the sweet and precious promises which are in him. Thus we are made partakers of the divine nature. 2 PETER 1:4. Hence we are one with God, garrisoned in God, kept by the power of God, obedient to the word of God, conformed to the image of God, and are sure and certain of the enjoyment of God. For his glory is engaged to fulfil all his promises. These faith receives from his word, and it works by love to all his holy precepts. O that our own faith may grow exceedingly, and our love abound. 2 THESSALONIANS 1:3.

Legality of spirit works by prodigality of heart; shuts out the love of Christ; brings in thraldom to the conscience, bondage to the soul, and shackles the feet from running the way of God's commands with delight. Sun of righteousness, cause thy glorious rays to dispel it. I through the law am dead to the law, that I might live unto God. GALATIANS 2:19.

We cannot honor the Son of God more, nor please the Father better, than by applying to him in the confidence of faith as the only Savior, under the most distressing sight, sense, and feeling of inbred sin, and of our lost state as sinners; seeing that he thus commands all such, Come unto me. MATTHEW 11:28.

Satan tempts to sin, accuses for sin, and aims to destroy our hope in Christ by sin. THE COMFORTER opposes the work and salvation of Christ in our consciences against all the aboundings of sin in us, and accusations of Satan against us; hereby he defeats Satan, and keeps up our confidence in Christ. The Spirit beareth witness to JESUS THE TRUTH, because the Spirit is truth. 1 JOHN 5:6.

How may one be sure that one has the faith of God's elect? Peter answers plainly, To you who believe, Christ is precious. 1 PETER 2:7. Is Christ precious to me? If so, his commands are not grievous, sin is hateful, the world contemptible, life vanity, death desirable, fellowship with Christ most estimable now, and the full enjoyment of Jesus in glory earnestly longed for. Come, Lord, in the power of thy Spirit, that as the panting hart longs for the cooling streams, so my soul may pant after thee, O God. PSALM 42:1.

Because our beloved Jesus is the beginning of our talk and the end of our conversation, the men who know him not cry, O you forget good works and morality of life, etc. Not so, no more than if we delighted to converse of the glory of the sun, we should be chargeable with denying its light, power, and influence. For it is the knowledge of Christ, love to Christ, the grace of Christ, and fellowship with Christ, which animates us to keep his commandments, and to do those things which are pleasing in his sight. 1 JOHN 3:22.

Though we cannot always rejoice in lively, comfortable frames of soul, yet we are commanded, Rejoice in the Lord always; and again I say, Rejoice. PHILIPPIANS 4:4. Be my frames ever so bad, my sorrows ever so many, and my corruptions ever so strong, yet He who once hung on the cross, and now dwelleth on high, is mightier than all: he is ever the same, his love changeth not, his compassions fail not, his salvation is everlasting, and his mercy endureth for ever. Though all in nature is dry, barren, and dead, yet I will rejoice in the Lord, I will joy in the God of my salvation. HABAKKUK 3:17, 18.

Would you enjoy much of God, be much in private with God: Ye are a habitation of God through the Spirit. EPHESIANS 2:22.

In the light of truth we see as much need to humble ourselves before God for the self-righteous pride of our hearts, which exalts itself against the grace of God, and rivals the glory of Christ, as for the licentiousness of our nature and rebellion of our will, which dishonor him. Lord, make me jealous over my heart for the former, and watchful against the latter; approving ourselves by the armor of righteousness on the right hand and on the left. 2 CORINTHIANS 6:7.

Many a towering professor's conscience is lulled into the sound sleep of carnal security, and is fondly dreaming of peace with God and safety in Christ, while the love of the world reigns in the heart, and the affections are set on things below. Most awful to read! The day of the Lord so cometh as a thief in the night. When they shall say, Peace and safety, then sudden destruction cometh upon them as travail upon a woman; and they shall not escape. 1 THESSALONIANS 5:2, 3. Examine yourselves; prove your own selves. 2 CORINTHIANS 13:5.

When we consider the infinite efficacy of the blood of the Son of God, which was shed for sin, we are apt to think all sinners will be saved. When we read in God's word of the holy hearts and holy lives of those who shall enter his kingdom, we are ready to cry out, Who then can be saved? And we must conclude with our Lord, Many are called, but few are chosen. MATTHEW 22:14. Narrow is the way that leadeth to life, and few there be who find it. MATTHEW 7:14. Give all diligence to make *your* calling and election sure. 2 PETER 1:10.

The gospel reveals the most ample provision for our comfort and holiness as lost sinners; but not the least encouragement to sin, or for pride and self-righteousness. To trust at all in our good works; to expect justification in any wise, in whole or in part, first or last, now or at the last day, by our obedience, is to exalt pride, to despise the gospel, to reject Christ, to neglect his great salvation, and to make the report of the life and death, the atonement and righteousness of the Son of God, no more than much ado about nothing. Obey your Lord's caution: Take heed and beware of the doctrine of the Pharisees. MATTHEW 16:6.

We know that in our flesh dwells no good thing. ROMANS 7:18. We find that our hearts are deceitful above all things, and desperately wicked. JEREMIAH 17:9. What then? Must we wait for hope, and refuse all comfort till we get a better opinion of ourselves? No, for grace reigns in the heart of God, through the righteousness of Christ, unto eternal life towards them in whom sin hath reigned unto death. ROMANS 5:21. Though sin abounds in us, yet grace does much more abound in Christ: Christ knows all that is in us better than we do or can. JOHN 2:25. Eternal praises to him. Because he knew we were lost, he came to seek and to save us. MATTHEW 18:11. Because he knew we were hopeless, he came to be our hope. 1 TIMOTHY 1:1. Because he daily sees that we are miserable by sin, and heavy-laden with sin, he lovingly invites, Come unto me, and sweetly promises, I will give you rest. MATTHEW 11:28. And because we are full of every discouragement in ourselves, he solemnly assures us, Him that cometh to me, I will in no wise cast out. JOHN 6:37. Let us take heed of getting a good opinion of ourselves, or thinking highly of ourselves as though we were, in ourselves, any thing but lost and hopeless sinners, who constantly need the blood of Christ to cleanse us, his righteousness to justify us, his tender heart to feel our infirmities, his powerful arm to save us, his fullness of grace to supply us, and his loving Spirit to guide and sanctify us. Let us be content to live by faith, as daily pensioners on his grace, and constant petitioners at his feet. Try Christ constantly: he is a tried stone always. ISAIAH 28:16. He ever lives to save to the uttermost. HEBREWS 7:25.

Were we only to look to Christ as our Priest, for pardon of sin, peace of conscience, and comfort of heart, without accepting him as our Prophet, to instruct us in his holy ways, and submitting to him as our King, to rule in our hearts, to reign over our lusts, and to bring all that is in us into subjection to himself, verily he might justly say to us, as he did to those of old, Ye only seek me for the loaves and fishes. JOHN 6:26. Lord, give me the heart of a disciple to follow thee unto death, as well as to believe on thee as a sinner unto justification of life. ROMANS 5:18.

To rest in past experiences is to indulge present sloth, and to nurse dead frames: it prevents coming to Christ for fresh life and liveliness, and creates suspicions whether they were really from God. Have we lost the comfort of past experiences? We cannot regain it by looking back on them, but by looking afresh to Christ, who died to redeem, rose to justify, and lives to pardon, refresh, and comfort us. For thus his loving heart proclaims to all his backsliding members, after the most base ingratitude and dreadful provocation: I have seen his ways, and will heal him; I will lead him also, and restore comforts unto him. ISAIAH 57:18.

Christ's question is of the greatest importance: When the Son of man cometh, shall he find faith on the earth? LUKE 18:8. Put this solemn question to thyself: Shall he find faith in me? Do I live by faith on him? Do I so believe his words as to obey his will? Do I take up his cross daily and follow him? Do I find all in him, so as to forsake all for him? Do I prefer Christ's cross to the world's glory, Christ's smiles to the world's frowns, Christ's commands to nature's lustings? Examine yourself by his word. Try your faith by his truth. Prove your love by obedience; for he saith, He that hath my commandments, and keepeth them, he it is that loveth me, etc. JOHN 14:21.

He who saith he hath no sin, nor any feeling of his corruptions, is in a state of perfect deadness. For being past feeling, through a deceived heart and a seared conscience, he cannot discern and say, Is there not a lie in my right hand? ISAIAH 44:20. Lord, make me to know myself, even as also I am known. 1 CORINTHIANS 13:12.

When I look at myself I am ashamed. When I look at God's holy law I am condemned. When I look at God's justice I despair. When I look into the gospel I grow bold; for I see pardon obtained, righteousness wrought out, salvation finished, and justice satisfied: then I am filled with hope. For God is just, and the justifier of him, even the ungodly, who believeth in Jesus. ROMANS 3:26.

The soul may enjoy peace with God amidst all the din of war from raging lusts, rebelling corruptions, a threatening world, and a roaring devil, if it abide in Jesus; for he saith, Peace I leave with you, my peace I give unto you. JOHN 14:27.

It is precious wisdom to distinguish between grace and nature, spirit and flesh, the old man and the new, the first man which is of the earth, earthly, and the second man which is the Lord from heaven, so as to separate the precious from the vile; for we are debtors, not to the flesh, to live after the flesh. ROMANS 8:12.

We too often consider our body of sin and death, instead of looking to Jesus, who bore our sins in his own body on the tree. Hence we grow weak in faith, and dejected in spirit. But we are called to follow the steps of our father Abraham, who considered not his own body, therefore staggered not at the promise of God through unbelief;

but was strong in faith, giving glory to God. ROMANS 4:20.

As sin is the one cause of condemnation unto death of
every son of man; so the righteousness of the Son of God
is the one cause of the justification of any son of man unto
life. ROMANS 5:18. Hence daily learn, O my soul, to humble
thyself before God for thy sins, and to rejoice in God for
the gift of righteousness by his beloved Son. ROMANS 5:17.

The bell tolls. A sinner is dead. Another soul is launched
into an awful eternity; is happy with Christ, or miserable
with Satan. Is Christ thy life, O my soul? has he the love
of thy heart? then fear not death; for he says, Whosoever
liveth and believeth in me, shall never die. JOHN 11:26.

If we have not always comfortable frames to rejoice in, yet
we have always THE LORD OUR RIGHTEOUSNESS to glory of. In
this LORD shall all the seed of Israel be justified, and shall
glory. ISAIAH 45:25. Blessed Spirit, take of the things of
Christ, show them unto me, and glorify him in my heart.

Religious disputes tend to promote irreligious passions.
Instead of edifying in the faith, they banish the peace of
God from the conscience, the love of Christ from the heart,
and compassion for one another from the soul. Contend
earnestly for the faith with the gentleness of love. Let all
your things be done with charity. 1 CORINTHIANS 16:14.

Those who trust in themselves that they are righteous,
and hold others, even the vilest of the vile, in contempt,
thinking them not so good, not so worthy of the divine
favor as themselves, are strictly and properly Pharisees,
our Lord himself being judge. LUKE 18. Whatever change
they may think is wrought in them, and which they
thank God for, is neither more nor less than a delusion
of their own self-righteous hearts, the offspring of pride
and ignorance, and comes from another spirit than the

Spirit of truth, the witness to, and the glorifier of Jesus; even from the father of lies, the enemy of all truth, Satan, whose working is with all deceivableness of unrighteousness in them that perish. Pray mind the reason: Because they received not the love of the truth, that they might be saved. 2 THESSALONIANS 2:10.

Hence, in all the life of the Son of God, we never once see him so severe against, nor denounce so many awful woes upon, even the worst and outwardly profligate sinners, as he did against persons of this proud stamp and self-righteous character. Yea, he positively declares, with this solemn asseveration, VERILY, I say unto you, publicans and harlots go into the kingdom of God before you. MATTHEW 21:31. From this spirit of pharisaic pride and self-righteousness we have all need to pray, Good Lord, deliver us. For though, through the riches of sovereign grace, we are not left under its reigning power, yet the leaven of it is in all our hearts, and is continually working in us, in opposition to that grace and truth which came by Jesus Christ, that righteousness for which Christ is the end of the law to every one who believes, and that hope of eternal life which is in him only for those who are in themselves unrighteous, hopeless, and lost.

God be merciful to me a sinner, is a suitable prayer for every sanctified believer. Lord, let me never forget my character as a sinner, nor thine, O Jesus, as the ONLY Savior. Let us come boldly to the throne of grace to obtain mercy. HEBREWS 4:16.

To walk with God is to live out of carnal sense, above corrupt reason, and contrary to the kingdom of nature and sin. It is to live by faith on Jesus, in whom God dwells, and is reconciled to, and at peace with every believer in his name; holding the mystery of faith in a pure conscience. 1 TIMOTHY 3:9.

Faith realizes to the soul, Christ, heaven, glory, and all objects invisible to sense; while it annihilates the world with all its vain enjoyments. In the power of thy grace and truth, dwell, O Holy Spirit, in my heart. Ye know the Spirit of truth, for he dwelleth with you, and shall be in you. JOHN 14:17.

The first Adam made me a sinner against God, therefore I will humble myself under the mighty hand of God. The second Adam hath made me righteous before God in his own spotless righteousness, therefore I will greatly rejoice in the LORD, *my* soul shall be joyful in *my* God, for he hath clothed *me* with the garments of salvation, he hath covered *me* with the robe of righteousness. ISAIAH 61:10. It is the Spirit that beareth witness, because the Spirit is truth. 1 JOHN 5:6.

Faith honors God's precious truth, exalts the riches of his grace, glorifies the Son of his love, trusts in the promises of his mercy, begets hope in the heart, brings peace in the conscience, works by love in the soul, and influences us desperate sinners to holiness of life. Hence we ascribe glory to God in the highest, and on earth peace, good will towards men. Well may faith be called PRECIOUS. Gracious Lord, increase my faith, and strengthen my soul by precious faith. 2 PETER 1:1.

When Jesus speaks in the power of his Spirit, and persuades the sinner's heart to believe his word, "I am the way," JOHN 14:6, he that moment repents of his folly in looking to any other way. He is humbled for his pride in walking in the way of his lusts and self-righteousness, and he abhors the many deceitful ways of men's devising. For that word makes him jealous with a godly jealousy over himself. There is a way which seemeth right to a man; but the end thereof are the ways of death. PROVERBS 16:25. As ye have received Christ Jesus the Lord, so walk ye in him,

COLOSSIANS 2:6, as poor needy sinners, daily looking to him to be a Savior from all sin, and Sanctifier unto holiness.

I will be good today, better tomorrow, and the third day I shall be perfect. Such is the dream of unawakened, self-righteous sinners. But the spiritually quickened soul says, I will continually flee to Jesus for refuge to lay hold of hope, to his blood for pardon, to his righteousness for justification, to his grace for sanctification, and to his finished salvation for eternal glory, that I may grow up into Christ in all things, who is my head. EPHESIANS 4:15.

Giving all diligence to the full assurance of hope unto the end, is the command of the Holy Ghost. HEBREWS 6:11. Yet how many expect to find the comfort of assurance who are not found in the way of diligence. Thou shalt not tempt the Lord thy God. MATTHEW 4:7. Dreadful charge! Ye do always resist the Holy Ghost. ACTS 7:51.

Never forget, Faith cometh by hearing, and hearing by the word of God. ROMANS 10:17. By the same means faith is begotten, it is strengthened and established. Faith sets prayer to work for its increase. Prayer employs faith for boldness. Faith begets hope for encouragement. Love accompanies faith and hope, and always comes attended with fear. And to crown all, the King of saints is ever present in that heart where these holy graces of his Spirit are. Then the soul cleaves and clings to him, and cries out in an ecstasy of joy, to which worldly and covetous hearts are strangers, My beloved is mine, and I am his; I held him, and would not let him go. SONG OF SOLOMON 2:16; 3:4. I am full; I have all, and abound. PHILIPPIANS 4:18. Lord, repeat thy visits.

The word of God is an infallible touchstone to try our graces. Bring them to this test, and it is an unerring standard to judge of our experiences. Examine yourselves by that; see if they spring from, and are agreeable to that: and then shall we have rejoicing in ourselves. GALATIANS 6:4.

God may say—and what if he should say this moment, Thy soul is required of thee? How stands it with thee? Art thou that fool who trusteth in his own heart? PROVERBS 28:26. Or art thou by the Scriptures made wise unto salvation through faith in Christ Jesus, so as to trust only in, and rely only upon the blood and righteousness of God's beloved Son, the justifier of the ungodly, and the Savior of sinners? If so, there is no condemnation to thee. ROMANS 8:1. Thy Lord, because he knows the working of unbelief in thee, assures thee with the solemn VERILY, VERILY, that thou art passed from death unto life, and shall not come into condemnation. JOHN 5:24. His watchword is, Fear not; for ye seek Jesus who was crucified. MATTHEW 28:5.

I have no time to read much, say many. No matter how little you read for your soul's good, unless of precious Christ, his great love and glorious salvation. Do you say, But I have no time to read of this; for I must mind the main chance? Then you most miserably kill time. The main chance! Now speak out the language of truth from your heart. Do not you also find that you have no time as you ought to think of Christ, pray to Christ, enjoy Christ, and to dwell on the coming of Christ? Remember, time is not thine own; it is only lent thee by thy Lord. Thou must account to him for it. As surely as you kill the love of Christ in your soul, time will kill your body. How dreadful, should Christ say to you in eternity, I have no time to think of you now! Redeem the time. EPHESIANS 5:16. It is high time to awake out of sleep. ROMANS 13:11. Spend more time to His glory who redeemed us, and you will find the profit of it. Less money and more of Christ would be best for thousands.

Fear of men, and shame for Christ, will shut our mouths from speaking for his glory, and contract our hearts in the enjoyment of his love. This shame is a bold enemy. This fear is a mighty conqueror. To live in shame, is to walk in terror and die in fear. To live under this fear, is to be shackled by shame, and die his prisoner. What is the only remedy against both? THE TRUTH. That is sufficient to arm us with courage against all the powers of earth and hell, even that Jesus made himself of no reputation, endured the cross, despising the shame, and is set down at the right hand of God. HEBREWS 12:2. The view of this amazing love to us, and suffering for us, will excite boldness in us, and drive cowardly shame and dastardly fear from us, while we ever remember what our dear Lord saith: Whosoever shall be ashamed of me and of my words in this adulterous generation, of him also shall the Son of man be ashamed when he cometh in the glory of his Father, with his holy angels. MARK 8:38.

Babes in Christ are apt to think most of their sparks of love to God. Fathers in Christ dwell most on God's everlasting love to them. Herein is love, not that we loved God, but that he loved us, and sent his Son to be the propitiation for our sins. We love him, because he first loved us. 1 JOHN 4:10, 19. Grow in grace, and in the knowledge of our Lord and Savior Jesus Christ. 2 PETER 3:18.

The duty of prayer is ours. Men ought always to pray, and not to faint, says our Lord. LUKE 18:1. But the spirit, life, and power of prayer, are from the Lord; let us not be slack in our duty to God, for he is not slack concerning his promise to us. 2 PETER 3:9.

The more confession of Christ, the more persecution for Christ. The more suffering for Christ's sake, the more enjoyment of Christ's love. This will ever be found true in experience. If we confess him, he also will confess us. If we suffer for him, we shall also reign with him. If we deny him, he also will deny us. 2 TIMOTHY 2:12.

It is the wisdom of a Christian not to be angry when rebuked, nor to be proud when praised. This is the remedy against both, Be clothed with humility. 1 PETER 5:5.

A Christian is not his own. His time is not at his own command; but he is ever to be at leisure for the service of his Lord, saying, Lord, what wilt thou have me to do? ACTS 9:6.

The men of this world trifle away their precious time, and their immortal souls. They know no better. But for one who professes to know the truth as it is in Jesus, to trifle with God's sacred truths and his own conscience, is to become, of all triflers, the most dreadful one. We have constant need to watch and pray, that we may be sincere and without offence till the day of Christ. PHILIPPIANS 1:10.

If we say that we have no sin, we deceive ourselves. 1 JOHN 1:8. If we aim to hide our sins from God, we vainly attempt to deceive him. If we confess our sins to him, plead the blood of Christ for pardon and cleansing before him, we disappoint Satan. For O encouraging promise from our Lord: Wherefore I say unto you, all manner of sin and blasphemy shall be forgiven unto men. MATTHEW 12:31.

Not all the floods of sin, nor all the waves of ungodliness, can ever extinguish the fire of God's love to his people in Christ. Yet the guilt of one single sin in the believer's conscience will raise a storm to the disturbance of his peace and terror of his mind. See then that ye walk circumspectly, not as fools, but as wise. EPHESIANS 5:15.

The sight and sense of indwelling sin beats down the pride of our heart. Then say some, "Let us do evil, that good may come: the more sin, the greater humility." Some presumptuous speakers and carnal reasoners know not the true grace of God wherein believers stand, and are strangers to godly sorrow for sin, which worketh evangelical repentance unto salvation. Of such Paul says, Whose damnation is just. ROMANS 3:8.

"Men may live fools, but fools they cannot die," says the poet. Indeed, but they both can and do die as great fools as they lived. Not grim death, but the holy Scriptures, are able to make us wise unto salvation, through faith in Christ Jesus. 2 TIMOTHY 3:15. Death may make men roar for their folly, but never administers one grain of soul-saving wisdom.

How many, having discharged thoughts of death, are now thinking within themselves, What shall I do? My trade flourishes; money comes in very fast. I must enlarge my shop, buy in more stock, increase my wealth, and I will say to my soul, Thou hast riches for many years to come; take thine ease, eat, drink, and be merry. But in such a moment we read of a brother of yours, to whom God said, Thou fool, this night thy soul shall be required of thee. LUKE 12:20. Aye, but say you, he was a fool indeed, for he knew nothing of the doctrines of grace. But I know and hear the gospel, and am convinced of the truth of the perseverance of the saints. That ought to yield you about as much consolation as though you had a scarlet cloak which he had not. For if your knowledge is greater, so is your condemnation. Our Lord gives us a double caution. Take heed and beware of covetousness, LUKE 12:15, and draws the contemptible character of a rich covetous fool, who was cut off in a moment in the midst of his wealth, and in the height of his folly. Riches were his idol, his soul was absorbed in covetousness, and unfit for death. How is it with you? Did you ever feel the force of our Lord's words? Did you ever tremble under his caution, Take heed and beware of covetousness? Did you ever feel its evil so as to cry fervently to him with Agur, Give me not riches? PROVERBS 30:8. Have you chosen God for your portion? Is your heart liberal to the poor? Can you meditate on death with pleasure, and expect it with a joyful hope in Jesus? If not, you are the very man to whom this parable belongs. Make not your knowledge a cloak for your covetousness. Each of the doctrines of grace is eternal truth. But so is this also, Covetousness is idolatry. COLOSSIANS 3:5. And ye know that no idolater hath any inheritance in the kingdom of Christ and of God. EPHESIANS 5:5.

Therefore what comfort can an idolater draw from this truth, that all the saints of God shall persevere in faith unto eternal glory, who has not the faith, heart, nor love of saints? Connecting a profession of the truth with the sin of covetousness is only adding deceit to sin. This, if lived in till death, will make a dying pillow very distressing, and the prospect of judgment most terrible. Oh death, how bitter is the remembrance of thee to a man who liveth at rest in his possessions, and who hath prosperity in all things! Oh death, how sweet is the remembrance of thee to the man in whose heart Christ dwells by faith; who has given up himself and his all to him in love; whose greatest honor is to obey his Lord, and whose greatest riches is to be rich towards God—rich in good works. Death will be the funeral of all his evils, and the resurrection of his unspeakable blessedness. For he shall be absent from his body of sin and death, and present with his Lord, who is his righteousness and life. Oh glorious appearing of our Savior Jesus Christ, who in our flesh hath abolished death, and brought life and immortality to light by the gospel. 2 TIMOTHY 1:10.

There are precious promises enough in God's blessed word to excite a joyful hope of our persevering in faith to the salvation of our souls. There are also awful warnings enough of others falling away, and making shipwreck of faith and a good conscience, to incite in us a godly jealousy over ourselves, lest we also fall away: let us labor therefore to enter into that rest, lest any man fall after the same example of unbelief. HEBREWS 4:11. Let him that thinketh he standeth, take heed lest he fall. 1 CORINTHIANS 10:12.

We fail in our duties of love, because we stagger at God's promises through unbelief. Lord, increase our faith, that love may abound, and obedience be cheerful.

Whenever we think the precepts of the gospel too strict, we may be sure we are straitened in our faith, and contracted in our love to Christ; and that the spirit of licentiousness works in us, in opposition to his truths. For faith makes *all* things possible. Love makes *all* things easy. Hope makes *all* things pleasant. Hence, because God worketh in us to will and to do, do *all* things without murmurings and disputings. PHILIPPIANS 2:13, 14.

Watchfulness is like a sentinel to the heart: it keeps out thieves and enemies, and admits none but friends to God and our souls, such as promote his glory and our good. Hear our Lord's words: I say unto all, WATCH. MARK 13:37.

A soldier of Christ fights every enemy under Christ's banner, having this motto, MORE THAN CONQUERORS THROUGH HIM THAT LOVED US. ROMANS 8:37. This inspires courage; for victory is sure.

These three things, ignorance, pride, and unbelief, nourish the life of self-righteous confidence in the heart; a fourth absolutely kills it—a sight of Christ by faith. While we behold the glory of God shining in the face of Jesus Christ, we are changed into the same image by the Spirit of the Lord. 2 CORINTHIANS 3:18.

Beware, lest at any time you make the doctrine of original sin and the total corruption of your nature the least plea for fulfilling the lusts of your flesh. But let it ever humble your pride, and excite you to cry to Jesus for salvation. For they that are Christ's have crucified the flesh, with its affections and lusts. GALATIANS 5:24. How shall we who are dead to sin, live any longer therein? ROMANS 6:2.

Had not Peter soared so high in self-confidence, he had not fallen so awfully low in lying, perjuring himself, and denying his Lord. A haughty spirit goeth before a fall. PROVERBS 16:18. This Peter woefully knew, therefore he earnestly exhorts, Be clothed with humility. 1 PETER 5:5.

Go not to any place where you cannot pray in faith, Lord, let thy presence go with me. Do nothing on which you cannot pray in hope, Lord, help me. Aspire after nothing for which you cannot ask in love, Lord, it is for thy glory, give it me. Whatsoever ye do in word and deed, do all in the name of the Lord Jesus. COLOSSIANS 3:17.

It is a very bad sign when professors of spiritual truths plead at all for carnal pleasures. At God's right hand are there not pleasures for evermore? PSALM 16:11.

It is good to know the sweet history of Christ's holy life, sin-atoning death, and glorious resurrection; blessed to know the mystery of it; and most joyful to experience that we are alive to him, dead to sin, and risen with him, through the faith of the operation of God. COLOSSIANS 2:12.

Peter had better have endured the coldness of his body without, than to have warmed himself by the high priest's fire within. For there the fire of temptations lighted up a hell in his conscience. Learn to be wise from others' harms. Indulgence to the body is often a snare to the soul. Endure hardness as a good soldier of Jesus Christ. 2 TIMOTHY 2:3.

Paul was, as every Christian is, like an insolvent debtor, who does not love to be at home, because he cannot face his creditors; therefore ever desires to be found in Christ, his surety, who has satisfied every demand of law and justice for him. This is the joyful claim of faith: Lord, thou art our dwelling-place. PSALM 90:1.

To walk by faith, is to view a reconciled God in Christ, simply taking him at his covenant word: Your sins and your iniquities I will remember no more. HEBREWS 10:17. This faith creates love to God, humility of heart, delight in holiness, and hatred of all sin. We love God, because he first loved us. 1 JOHN 4:19.

As Christians, our one grand business is to know the preciousness of Christ, to live in the fellowship of God, and to walk in the comforts of the Holy Ghost. Hence, it should be our chief study to use all means conducive hereto, and to avoid all things contrary to this. But it is amazing to hear professors ask, What harm is there in this? What evil in that? What hurt in another thing? Harm, evil, and hurt! Surely all is so that is not edifying in the faith, promotive of love, and conducive to holiness. If the scenes of the playhouse, the diversions of the card-table, and the joys of carnal company are profitable to these, then pursue them with eagerness. But ever remember, WHATSOEVER is not of faith, is SIN. ROMANS 14:23. That soul is in a right frame, and walks in the light of truth, who says, Were I as meek as Moses, as patient as Job, as loving as John, and as zealous as Paul, yet with him I would confess myself the chief of sinners, renounce my own righteousness, glory only in the righteousness of Christ, and desire to be found in him in life, in death, and at the throne of grace now, and before the judgment-seat at the last day. Behold, his soul which is lifted up—with what he is in himself—is not upright in him; but the just shall live by his faith, HABAKKUK 2:4—live by what his faith brings into his heart and conscience from the word of truth, concerning the righteous life and sin-atoning death of his Savior. We are the true circumcision, who rejoice in Christ Jesus, and have no confidence in the flesh. PHILIPPIANS 3:3.

To make the heart truly happy, and the life really holy, love and fear must be united. If we love to enjoy the comfort of the precious truths of God, we must fear to transgress the holy commands of God. Be thou in the fear of the Lord all the day long. PROVERBS 23:17.

The disdainful irony, contemptuous sneer, and indignant frown of the world never killed the life of any one Christian. But by its alluring smiles, specious promises, and bewitching charms, many a professor has been hugged to death. Marvel not if the world hate you. 1 JOHN 3:13.

FAITH views all in Christ. HOPE expects all from Christ. LOVE gives up all for Christ. The nourishment of faith, hope, and love, is the word of Christ. Let the word of Christ dwell in you richly. COLOSSIANS 3:16.

Does any poor sinner ask, Where shall I find God, to the peace of my conscience, the comfort of my heart, and the joy of my soul? The Holy Spirit bears witness that the Godhead, the fullness of the Godhead, yea, all the fullness of the Godhead, dwells in Christ. COLOSSIANS 2:9. A God out of Christ is the idol of ignorance. God in Christ reconciled to sinners, is the revealed object of truth, and glory of faith. They shall all be taught of God. JOHN 6:45.

Be not idle as to the means of grace; but be careful not to make an idol of the means. Use means as if they were all; yet look through the means as though they were nothing at all, to Christ, who is above all, and in all. He is altogether lovely. SONG OF SOLOMON 5:16.

Though it be cursed to worship the virgin Mary, yet it is blessed to imitate her in keeping all the sayings of Jesus in our hearts, from his first saying, I must be about my Father's business, LUKE 2:49, till he cried with his expiring breath, It is finished. JOHN 19:30. His Father's business was to fulfil his holy law, and to save his beloved people. Am I one? Jesus tells you, If a man love me, he will keep my words, and my Father will love him, and we will come unto him, and make our abode with him. He who loveth me not, keepeth not my sayings. JOHN 14:23, 24.

When any one troubles you with importunity, beware of impatience. Remember how troublesome you are to God, and how long-suffering and patient he is with you. Put on, as the elect of God, holy and beloved, bowels of mercies, kindness, humbleness of mind, etc. COLOSSIANS 3:12.

Though it be cursed work to make Christ's righteousness and the liberty of the gospel a cloak for a life of licentiousness; yet it is the blessedness of faith to walk in the liberty of the gospel, and to receive the righteousness of Christ as a glorious robe to hide our deformity, and to cover our iniquity from the view of divine justice. Blessed is the man whose sin is covered, to whom the Lord imputeth righteousness without works. ROMANS 4:5, 6.

Though no one truth in Scripture is made true by our believing it, yet the truth becomes saving to our souls by faith. And without faith we can enjoy no benefit of hope, nor receive any comfort of salvation from gospel truths; yea, without the belief of the truth as it is in Jesus, we are under the sentence of the law, of curse, wrath, and damnation. He that believeth not, shall be damned. MARK 16:16. Consider these truths: The Lord hath laid the iniquity of us all upon Christ. ISAIAH 53:6. Christ himself bore our sins in his own body on the tree, and by his stripes we are healed. 1 PETER 2:24. Now do you believe this fact, testified by the Spirit; of truth, from two witnesses, his prophet and apostle? If so, why should you bear the burden of sin on your mind; the guilt of sin on your conscience, and a dread of punishment of sin on your heart one moment? You will not, you cannot, if you really believe this truth in your heart. For as soon as this live coal of truth, taken off the altar of Christ's sacrifice, touches the heart, lo, our iniquity is taken away, and our sin is purged. ISAIAH 6:6, 7.

Every doctrine of grace is a plea for the prayer of faith. The pleas of faith please God, honor his truth, and bring the grace and power of his doctrines into lively experience in the soul. Thus we are made lively in faith, joyful in hope, comfortable in love, and obedient in life. Put me in remembrance: let us plead together. ISAIAH 43:26. This is our Lord's precious command. Let us not neglect our duty. Pride and poverty make a most contemptible character. Such is ours. Though in most extreme indigence, yet we are naturally too proud to dig in the field of the gospel for supply, and ashamed to beg mercy at the feet of Christ as miserable. We are content to go to hell with proud self-righteous notions, rather than to be beholden to God's grace and Christ's salvation. But— Oh blessed 'but!'—but God, who is rich in mercy, for his great love wherewith he loved us, even when we were dead in sins, hath quickened us together with Christ, etc. EPHESIANS 2:4, 5. Most amazingly rich mercy! most astonishingly great love! when dead in sins, blinded by pride to our wretchedness, and full of enmity against God and goodness, even then he loved us with great love, and of rich mercy quickened us. O look at, live, and feed upon this rich mercy and great love. Consider what God hath done for you. Talk no more arrogantly of free-will pride, of any pious notions, good purposes, and holy resolutions of yours. Grace prevented all, rich mercy was prior to all, great love was before all. Oh, to grace what mighty debtors! Your glorying in pride and self-righteousness is not good. Purge out therefore the old leaven. 1 CORINTHIANS 5:7.

Christ's followers are not like travellers who are frequently at a stand, and know not their way. But Christ saith, The way ye know: I am the way. JOHN 14:4, 6. And they reply, We are in him that is true. 1 JOHN 5:20. They are sure of it. They are brought out of the broad way of sin and self-righteousness. They are in the way of the Father's love, in the way of his Son's salvation, in the way of the Spirit's joy and peace. They have access to God's throne, and acceptance to his heart, being made accepted in his beloved Son. They are walking in the highway of holiness, life, and salvation, which shall soon terminate in the endless fruition of God in glory. And all this is to the praise of the glory of God's grace. EPHESIANS 1:6. He who cannot see this is blind to Christ, who is the way, the truth, and the life. The way of a fool is right in his own eyes; but he that hearkeneth unto counsel—the word of truth—is wise. PROVERBS 12:15. The Scriptures are able to make us wise unto salvation. 2 TIMOTHY 3:15. O for more love to them, and daily delight in searching them.

O my soul, when thou feelest with sorrow the sin and misery of thy first birth into nature, reflect with joy on thy second birth into Christ. Give glory to God the Father, who of his own will begat thee with the word of truth, JAMES 1:18; to God the Spirit, who quickened thee, when dead in trespasses and sins. EPHESIANS 2:1. Rejoice in and glory in God the Son, into whom thou wast born again, and hast a lively hope by his resurrection from the dead. 1 Peter 1:3.

Despair in self kills nature's pride. Write despair on all you are, and all you can do to make yourself righteous before God, to justify yourself in the sight of God, and to entitle yourself to the favor and kingdom of God. But ever beware of giving the least way to despondency of God's grace in his Son, and of his truth revealed by his Spirit; for the least kind of this despair preys upon the soul, rankles the conscience, eats into the joy of faith, the comfort of hope, the consolation of love, and every heavenly influence to holy obedience. This is the Christian's motto: Perplexed, but not in despair. 2 CORINTHIANS 4:8. We are made partakers of Christ, or Christ's partners in his heavenly inheritance, if we hold the beginning of our confidence steadfast unto the end. HEBREWS 3:14. Lord, comfort my heart, and establish me in every good word and work. 2 THESSALONIANS 2:17.

We can never walk comfortably, run patiently, fight valiantly, resist Satan steadfastly, strive against sin powerfully, pray fervently, hope joyfully, and obtain victory completely, but while we are looking to Christ, THE CAPTAIN OF OUR SALVATION. HEBREWS 2:10.

Give up ALL for Christ, and you shall enjoy ALL in Christ. It is the fullness of Christ that filleth all in all. EPHESIANS 1:23.

Had I this hour the solemn prospect of death, were I this moment launching into an awful eternity, what, O my soul, hast thou to look to, to trust in, and to plead? Through thy help, O Holy Spirit, I would look to nothing, rest on nothing, trust in nothing, plead nothing but the perfect work of my precious Lord, of which with his dying breath he proclaimed, IT IS FINISHED. JOHN 19:30.

Have you contracted fresh guilt upon your conscience? Fly instantly to Christ's blood for fresh cleansing, that you may have fresh comfort, and Christ get fresh glory; for Christ receiveth us to the glory of God. ROMANS 15:7.

To trust in one's good frames and fine feelings, to live upon them, and to pride ourselves in them, is natural to us. But this is the sure way to lose them. To be content with bad frames and uncomfortable feelings, is to live at a distance from the fire of God's love and the beams of the

Sun of righteousness. Woe be unto them who are settled upon their lees, and say in their heart, The Lord will not do good, neither will he do evil. ZEPHANIAH 1:12.

Do you see yourself a great sinner? Then never think of the GREAT GOD without adding even our Savior Jesus Christ, and remembering, He gave himself for us. TITUS 2:13, 14. For the thought of a great God without being our Savior, and giving himself for us, will strike you with hopeless terror.

The end of all things is at hand; the great day of the Lord is near: then, for despising the glorious gospel, rejecting precious Christ, and neglecting his great salvation, sinners must give an awful account unto him as their Judge. For Christ shall be revealed from heaven, in flaming fire taking vengeance on them who know not God, and that obey not the gospel of Christ. 2 THESSALONIANS 1:8. There is no knowing God, but by the gospel of Christ. This tremendous day we may think of with pleasure, look for with joy, and welcome with triumph, if we believe the gospel, receive Christ, trust in his salvation, and walk in his love. For he shall come to be glorified in his saints, and to be admired in all who believe, in that day. VERSE 10. O believer, why grovel in sense? why dejected in spirit? why live below thy privilege? Look unto, meditate on, delight in thy God in thy flesh, thy glory, the Author and Finisher of our faith, HEBREWS 12:2, the end of the law for righteousness. ROMANS 10:4. He who hath said of our salvation, IT IS FINISHED, JOHN 19:30, is in you the hope of glory, COLOSSIANS 1:27, and assures you, I will come again, and receive you unto myself; that where I am, there ye may be also. JOHN 14:3. Till then, hear thy Lord in faith; honor his truth; obey him in love; look up in hope. Lift up your heads with joy, for your redemption draweth nigh. LUKE 21:28.

www.ingramcontent.com/pod-product-compliance
Lightning Source LLC
Chambersburg PA
CBHW021141020426
42331CB00005B/856